MW01025733

I Don't Need No Scruples

Michael Howlett

ISBN 9781490488448

Dedicated to all who have played a role in the warping of my mind, but most especially Dr. Hunter S. Thompson, Tom Robbins, and Kurt Vonnegut, Jr.

On Imagination

And God saw that the wickedness of man was great in the earth, and that every imagination of the thoughts of his heart was only evil continually." Genesis 6:5

Table of Contents

I Don't Need No Scruples

Back in the saddle

Little did I know when the family and I went on an outing to Foster Falls State Park that I would come back from the experience a changed man. Little did I know that the tale of my exploits that fateful morning would spread through the camp faster than fire through a meth lab.

After finding our campsite, we immediately headed to the stables. The Mistress of the Manor, my grandson and my son-in-law had never ridden a horse. My daughter had not ridden a horse since she was maybe eight, and the last time I mounted a steed (hey, stop the sniggering) I was around 15. So, we were all anxious to saddle up and test our equestrian skills.

Things started fine. We mounted our appointed horses and began our trek through the park, riding along slowly and enjoying the beauty of our surroundings. We had only been riding for a short while when we heard the sound of a horse galloping quickly up from behind us. In a blur, a horse shot past us, as if fleeing from a posse of Elmer's Glue employees. Clinging to the out-of-control horse was a young lady, who was screaming wildly.

Being the most advanced rider of our group, I felt it was I who must save the damsel in distress. I gave my horse a kick 1off I went. As I rode up beside the frenzied maiden, I reached for the reins of her horse, which were flapping wildly. However, I misjudged the distance, and as I reached for the reins, I found myself falling. I did manage to grab the reins before I hit the ground, which jerked the horse to a stop. I stopped when I hit the ground. So, now I'm left with an extremely sore back, and possibly a fractured rib or two. But, it was well worth it since I was able to save the young lady from possibly a more disastrous fate.

It didn't take long before my fame spread throughout the park, and — what? That's not the way you heard it? Well, I may have taken a few liberties, but — what? You heard there was no young lady on a runaway horse? Well, okay, I may have made that part up, but… okay, okay, that's not exactly the way it happened.

Before mounting our horses (hey, I said stop the sniggering), we put on our bicycle helmets, which I credit with the cause of the whole incident. Who can properly ride a horse when wearing a helmet, rather than a cowboy hat? That will shake anyone's confidence. The park ranger then asked, "Who has the most experience?" I proudly spoke up and was directed to a brown-and-white horse that looked peaceful enough, but, I now know, was the spawn of Satan. I don't remember the name of the horse, but I will refer to it, now and forever, as Sphincter.

Anyway, I placed my foot in the stirrup and attempted to mount (this is the last time I'm saying it, stop the sniggering) Sphincter. My first attempt failed, but I gave it another shot, which also failed. It should be noted that my left knee, my mounting knee, is, to use a medical term, "screwed up." It does not bare weight very well and sometimes locks up. When I reach Medicare age, if there is to be such a thing in the future, I will have it repaired.

Since two attempts to saddle up had failed, the park ranger suggested I use a set of steps used by children, midgets and those people with the agility of a one-legged barn monkey. Well, this seemed simple enough. I was so elevated that I figured I didn't even need to put my foot in the stirrup, and I threw my leg across the saddle. It was then Sphincter decided to shift a little. All of a sudden, my rear end was no longer above the saddle, but beside my malicious, tick-infested excuse for equine gentility. My grip on the saddle horn wasn't enough to secure my 230-some pounds and down I went. If I had hit the ground clean, I think I would have been okay. Embarrassed, sure, but not injured. However, that is not what happened. When I went down, I planted my back, and I think, my kidneys, firmly on the steps. As I rolled over in agony, I looked up at Sphincter. He was staring at me with a look that not only showed his disdain for me, but said, if he could talk, "Bite me, Cowboy."

Then the park ranger asked if I was okay. I replied, "I don't know yet," because I expected to find a kidney, and quite possibly, a spleen lying in the dirt. She walked me back into the office and applied disinfectant to the foot-long abrasions running down my lower back. She continued to ask me if I was okay, and then had me sign an accident report. I didn't read it, but I knew Sphincter would not receive any of the blame for this.

We spent the rest of the day at the park, and had a good time. However, I could not frolic in the river, or ride a canoe, or do anything that required me to move quicker than a quadriplegic sloth. As we left for the day, the Mistress of the Manor wanted to go by the stables and say goodbye to Dakota, her well-trained and non-evil horse. I said I would prefer to visit the stables on another trip, when I am back to full health, if ever I am, because I had a grudge to settle with Sphincter. His day is coming.

Beware strange co-workers

I was recently reading an article entitled "seven habits that are secretly driving your co-workers crazy." Now, there were certainly some annoying habits on the list, most of which I have encountered in my over 30 years in the field of journalism. But — isn't there always a but — there was one bizarre habit exhibited by a former co-worker that beat them all. A number of years ago we had a young man working as a reporter who one might describe as "troubled," "strange," or "special." In truth, he was crazier than a werewolf with psoriasis.

One day, Dennis, the paper's circulation manager, came over to a group of us, who were, of course, discussing important journalism issues, such as Final Four brackets or the most recent movies we had seen, and, with a sense of urgency, said, "You won't believe what just happened to me!" Since I had been in the newspaper business for quite a while at that point, I didn't really think what he had to say would surprise me, but I was wrong.

Dennis said when he opened the door to the men's restroom, he found the aforementioned young man standing in an open stall completely naked, his neatly folded clothes lying on the floor. As one might expect, Dennis got the heck out of there. Now, if this had been a one-time occurrence, then we might have written it off as say, the young man was just checking for ticks. However, it happened a second time, again to Dennis, who then began driving to the nearest public restroom rather than risk another strange encounter.

The young man's quirks didn't stop there. We had a TV in the newsroom so as to help us keep abreast of breaking news and, of course, to watch basketball and football games. Now, the young man, as it turned out, had a Brady Bunch fetish. Each evening at 7 p.m. while we were working, he would ask if he could turn the TV to the channel that broadcast that miserable show. If we refused, we were afraid he might just strip down there in the newsroom, so we would usually let him watch the Brady Bunch, unless, of course, there was a basketball or football game on. Then, well, we just took our chances.

As far as the list goes, I think this young man falls under the category of "doing things that gross people out." Luckily, he wasn't with us long; just long enough to become a legend in the annals of strange co-workers.

Another young man who worked at the paper did a very good job, but had a habit of blurting out important questions such as "If King Kong and Godzilla got in a fight, who would win?" Well, of course, Godzilla, but that's beside the point. Most of the time, this was not a problem, since we were all journalists, we naturally had inquiring minds, so the question of who would win this epic bout was certainly of interest to us.

At other times, he would burst out in song, with The Rolling Stones' "Jumpin' Jack Flash" being one of his favorites.

Now, anyone who knows me knows I love The Stones, so most of the time this too was okay. The only problem was it didn't matter if it was 5 p.m. or 30 minutes before our midnight deadline, when he got the urge to sing or pose an interesting question, he did. Now, what's fun and entertaining at 5 p.m. is often a major pain in the butt 30 minutes before a midnight deadline.

Yes, working in an office with a whole bunch of people leads to some interesting encounters. Some may be too touchy-feely, some may smell bad and some may borrow items without asking. However, you can count yourself lucky if these are the worst things you have to deal with. Remember, you could one day walk into the restroom only to find a co-worker stripped down to nothing. Worst yet, he could also be singing the Brady Bunch theme song.

Vacating with mermaids

Well, folks, summer is just around the corner, and we all know what that means – vacation time. Soon, many of you will be frolicking in the waves of various beaches, or cursing about the six-hour wait in line at Disney World, or lying in a wading pool in the backyard. Then there are those who want something different, something out of the ordinary; something they will remember for the rest of their lives.

With that in mind, I have found an article concerning vacations that will blow your mind, lift your spirits and tickle your fancy, and who doesn't like to have their fancy tickled? I know I sure do. Now, these suggestions aren't for the timid soul, no siree, these are vacations for the adventurous, for the wild at heart, for the drunk out of their minds.

Say you've always wanted to swim with mermaids, but have never gotten the chance. Well, it's here, but maybe not for long, so you had better get your flippers in gear and head to Florida. It seems Weeki Wachee Springs, which allows you to swim with mermaids, has fallen on hard times. A police raid put it out of business for a while, something about illegal flipper dances, but it's trying to make a comeback. Now, these aren't your Disney cartoon character mermaids, no these are the real bubble-blowing deal, if you know what I mean. So, if you don't want the poor mermaids kicked to the surf, you need to visit. Since many seafaring men believe that a mermaid's only purpose is to lead men to their deaths, you might want to give this one some careful thought.

Maybe mermaids aren't your thing. Maybe you're nuts. Who wouldn't want to swim with mermaids? Still, there is another option, this one for all the animal lovers. If you think I'm talking about swimming with dolphins, you are sadly mistaken. Everybody's done that. No, this much worse. If you head to Big Major Cay, also in Florida, you can swim with their paddling porcine, otherwise known as pigs. If you're like me, you're thinking why in the world would anybody want to swim with pigs. I love bacon, but swimming with it is ridiculous.

Now, if you are really, really adventurous, you might want to visit Australia, where you can vacate in a 7x10x7-foot tomb, at least that's what I call it. The guy who had it built spent 12 days in that little bit of hell and now he wants to share it with the world. Not only, are you submerged in a flooded gravel pit, but also, you have to ride a bike to generate electricity and use algae soaked in your own urine to produce oxygen. It doesn't get any better than that.

If the thing you hate about vacations is all that packing and unpacking, and the airline losing your luggage, well, maybe you should try a *nakation*. All you need to pack is sunscreen, lots and lots of sunscreen, sunglasses and sandals. You're probably thinking that I'm forgetting something, but I'm not. You see a *nakation* is what professional vacation planners call a vacation that involves nudity. I'm not talking about private nudity, no, no, no. I'm talking about public nudity, like other-people-will-see–you-naked- nudity. It turns out this kind of thing is catching on, even in Puritanical America. Last year, a poll revealed that only 31 percent of Americans would be willing to bare it all in public, but this year the figure is up to 48 percent. The bad part of that statistic is, of the 48 percent who would go nude in public, there were only 11 percent of them anybody wanted to see nude.

Now, I've saved the best two for last. And by that, I mean either one could be the last vacation you ever take. I don't know who came up with the idea that a trip to Afghanistan would make for a good vacation, but somebody did. Although the article points out that the country isn't necessarily safe for tourists at the moment, it still attempts to lure you there by talking about The City of Screams, the Minarets of Ghazni, the Blue Mosque and breathtaking landscapes. When a description of a vacation includes both City of Screams and breathtaking in the same sentence; I usually mark that one off my list. I don't want any screaming or breathtaking on my vacation, especially the breathtaking.

The final vacation recommended is a space adventure, and we're not talking Space Mountain here. No, we're talking a Soyuz spacecraft. For a mere $100 million, you and your sweetie can enjoy a seven-day space flight. You will speed along at 17,000 mph and be able to view the Earth from 250,000 miles in space. Candidates must train for four months, alongside Russian cosmonauts, at the Yuri Gagarin Cosmonaut Training Center in Star City, Russia, which is a vacation in itself if you like being bossed around by Russkies.

Now, I spent almost two years in Alaska as part of the U.S. Army protecting this country from the evil Russkies, and, I'm proud to say that not one Russkies tank, not one Russkies missile, not one Russkies evil genius broke through our defenses. Fighting evil Russkies is in my blood, training with them is right out. I'm also going to pass on Afghanistan, living in a tomb and swimming with paddling porcine. However, I think I might like to combine two of the other vacation ideas by swimming naked with the bubble-blowing mermaids of Weeki Wachee Springs … wait … okay … I've just been told by the Mistress of the Manor that the closest I'm getting to a bubble-blowing mermaid is a wading pool in our backyard. Oh well, a fellow can dream.

Sweet smelling underpants

Fragrances are big business worldwide. We humans want everything to smell good – our clothes and sheets, our candles, our lotions and creams, our homes and cars, and, especially, our bodies. Good smells are a $14 billion a year industry.

Now, of course, there are humans who don't care about smelling good, and most of them are of my gender. In fact, I know one man who revels in his foulness. You might know him; he goes by the name of Rooster Edwards. I once asked Rooster why he always smells like the inside of a gutted marmoset that has been lying in the hot sun for a week, and he told me it was the only way he could keep Ugina, his wife, from pawing him. Rooster fancies himself a ladies' man, but Ugina is the only female who has ever willingly stayed in the same room alone with Rooster, for more than five minutes, much less pawed him.

Now, society has been trying to clean men like Rooster up since Urgh killed his first mammoth and, as was the custom of the Smrk tribe, rolled around inside the slaughtered animal's remains. It is no coincidence that the Smrks didn't last long, since the females of the tribe decided it was better to die out than rut with males who smelled of mammoth intestines.

The efforts to improve manly hygiene got a boost during the Disco era and continued picking up steam until the term *metro sexual* was coined in 1994 to describe a man who is especially meticulous about his grooming and appearance. There are now way too many web sites dedicated to helping men look pretty and smell good. One of these is The Art of Manliness, which has a drawing of a bare-knuckle fighter on its masthead. I'm not sure what the fighter has to do with looking good and smelling pretty, unless it's saying it's okay to offend people by punching them, but it's not okay to make them hurl because of your smell.

One of the articles on that web site is "5 Products No Man's Bathroom Should be Without." I thought a toilet would be at the top of the list and a shower close behind, but neither one made the list. However, Gold Bond Body Powder did. The article says the powder should be "applied to hot spots to keep them comfortable." Now, if there is one thing I like to keep comfortable, it's my hot spots.

The web site also has other must-read articles, such as "How to Grow a Handlebar Moustache," "A Men's Guide to Overcoats," and "How to Roll up Your Shirt Sleeves." I found that last article very interesting; you see, I have been sleeve-challenged my entire life. Those darn sleeves are so tricky that it's virtually impossible to roll them up properly without guidance. I wanted to take a course in sleeve rolling in college, but it was so popular I could never to get into the class, so I have had to slouch through life with improperly rolled sleeves, bringing disgrace and shame to my family. However, thanks to this article, I can now be a true Renaissance man.

One of the other must-haves on the list is cologne. Here we are again trying to make men smell good. Of course, cologne has been around forever, on the face, on the neck, under the armpits, quite possibly near a hot spot. But now, there's a much easier way for men to keep their hot spot smelling like roses, daises or even apricots.

Yes, siree, thanks to Guilllaume Gibault, Le Sip Francais will soon be selling scented men's underpants. These magical underpants will hold a fresh scent for up to 30 washes, so they are not a one-time thing like edible underwear. These babies last. Gibault has assured critics that the "musk and pear scents are rather masculine and not too strong." Thank God, if there is one thing I can't stand, it is for my hot spot to smell too musky. I already have that problem.

Now, if you're thinking about buying these wonders of manufacturing, you should know sweet smelling underpants don't come cheap – briefs are $46 and boxers are $53. Heck, I don't spend that much money on underpants in five years' time.

However, if I do decide to give scented underwear a go, I don't think musk or pear will be my choice. No, if I'm going to be sweet smelling like society wants me to, I think I'll go with banana, coconut or, quite possibly, honeysuckle.

Why don't countries like us?

Ever wonder which countries hate the United States the most. Many countries hate us, but we really can't help it. We were just born with a strong personality and, quite possibly, a bi-polar disorder. Nevertheless, we are hated, that's for sure. Either other countries want us to stay out of their business, or they want us to interfere and we won't. We can't win. As one might expect, most of the haters are in the Middle East, but we also have haters in Europe and Africa.

Although they didn't make the list, I'm pretty sure Canada isn't all that pleased with us most of the time, but they're just too polite to say anything. You would think Canada would have a bolder personality, but, apparently, British civility has proved dominant over its other two influences, U.S. pushiness and French rudeness.

Our other neighbor, Mexico, however, loves us, it wants us to be its boyfriend, it wants us to marry it. The main thing it wants, however, is jobs and government assistance.

As far as I can tell, there are only two other countries that really like us, and they are, of course, Britain and Israel, and sometimes I question Israel. Yes, we can always count on the support of the British no matter what fool war or economic crisis we get them into, and Israel has to be our friend because who else will have their back if something nasty goes down?

Now, there is one continent that loves us, but, then again, it loves everybody, and that is Antarctica. One reason it likes us is because there are no Antarcticans, just penguins and some birds whose inner compass has failed. Heck, Antarctica is just glad somebody will visit it.

Okay, back to the haters. Before we go any further, however, everybody needs to make a list of their top five, so as to ascertain just how astute you are about which countries hate the U.S. the most. I'm sure a lot of you put Iran right on top of the list, but, my good sirs and madams, you would be wrong. No siree, Iran comes sixth on the list. In fact, we are making advances with the Iranians. Already 12 percent like us, as opposed to just nine percent two years ago. If we keep this up, by 2037 the majority of Iranians will like us. The remainder will, however, still want to feed us to their goats.

How many put Greece on their list? Nobody? Well, believe it, or not, Greece is ninth on the list. The Grecians, apparently, blame us for their lousy economy. We've tried to tell them, "do what I say, not what I do." They won't listen. They just go around dancing on their roofs and playing their fiddles like life is a bowl of Baklava.

Serbia, No. 10, and Algeria, a surprising No. 3, are none too happy with the good old U.S.A. Serbia dislikes us because we took Kosovo's side in its decision to break it off with Serbia, which was rumored to be cheating with Albania, a slut if there ever was one, while Algeria is … well Algeria. They've always had an attitude problem.

Yemen and Iraq come in at eighth and seventh, respectively, while Egypt ranks fifth and Lebanon fourth on the list of U.S. haters. What surprises me is Lebanon being on the list. It's been so quiet lately that I didn't even realize it was still a country.

That brings us to the top two on the charts. The runner-up is the Palestinian Territories, who hate us because we are Israel's BFF, and No. 1 with a bullet, for just about every American I might add, is Pakistan, which still accepts our aid with open arms. In fact, 79 percent of Pakistanis hate the U.S. That number was already high, but that little rumble with Osama really ticked a lot more of them off. Of course, they weren't really our friends anyway. They just liked us because we have money to spread around and throw awesome parties.

After going over the list, I've tried to think just how we can increase our popularity. Well, we already put out more than a $5 hooker, so that can't be it. Maybe, we just need a positive ad campaign, something like, "Hey, world, let's hang out together," or "We let our friends borrow missiles and stuff."

Odors on a plane

I was reading an article entitled "The Nine Most Common Airplane Accidents" and was quiet surprised that crashing and exploding into a massive ball of flame was not among them. You see, when I fly, that's what I expect to happen.

Now, I know that flying is safer than driving a car, at least that's what the airline companies say; but there is seldom an automobile accident in which a car drops 30,000 feet, so I'd rather take my chances in a car. Plus, airplanes don't have individual airbags.

I have good reason for my fear of flying, even though I had it before I had actually flown. My last two flights, things didn't go well. I flew all the way across this great country to Seattle, then up to Anchorage, without anything more than a little turbulence. But when it came to flying from Bristol to Louisville and back again, all hell broke loose.

The flight to Louisville took place in the morning, so as soon as we reached the proper altitude, the stewardesses began serving coffee, orange juice and such. Then all of a sudden, the 727 nosedived for what seemed like a lifetime; I say that because I thought my life was over. Drinks and food flew everywhere; the stewardesses and any passengers on their feet were thrown to the front of the plane, and screaming was abundant. After the plane pulled out of the dive and leveled off, I politely asked a stewardess what happened. She hesitated and answered, "Turbulence." I answered back, "The hell it was!" Actually, I said much more than that, but decency prohibits me from subjecting readers to my full tirade.

Since the flight to Louisville was such a terror that the purchase of some new underpants was required, I figured the trip back to Bristol would be much better. I was wrong. However, it wasn't the flight this time, but the landing. We came in for the landing and before you could yell Amelia Earhart, we were going back up. A second attempt failed before the pilot managed to land the plane on the third attempt. When we taxied around, one wing was hovering over grass. You see, why I am not a fan of flying.

Okay, back to the most common accidents. Some, you would expect — turbulence, landing gear problems, bird strikes and engine problems — but there were a couple I didn't expect, like odors and lasers. Five times since 2010, odors on commercial flights have caused not only illness, but also hospitalization and have even forced flights to be diverted or to make quick landings. In each case, the odor is still unknown or still being investigated. The FFA has attributed the problems to an "unknown substance on board." No offense to the geniuses at the FFA, but Rooster Edwards could have done better than that.

You might think that leaving Mexican food off the flight menu might solve the problem, but, apparently, the problem goes deeper than the bowels. I'm thinking we've got an X-Files case here, but I could be wrong — well, there's a slight possibility, anyway. I'm not sure what is emitting these noxious fumes, although cabbage could be involved, but I'm thinking sabotage, most probably by that nut job, the one I like to call "Monkey Boy," who runs North Korea. The public threats of nuclear missile attacks are a ploy to divert our attention from the real threat, biological warfare.

The lasers that are causing problems are not the ones that blow up Godzilla, no, these are of the laser pointer variety ... you know, the ones students use to highlight their teacher's nipples during class, or to shine in an opposing player's eyes during a basketball game. So what's all the fuss about laser pointers? Well, they're dangerous!

Between 2010 and 2013, laser pointers caused injuries on three different commercial flights. In two of the flights, a pilot sustained eye injuries, while a member of the flight crew sustained an eye injury in the other. In fact, one of those incidents got a young man 30 months in prison. Yes, it's all fun and games until someone loses an eye. Isn't that what mother used to say? Well, chalk one up for mom.

Now, I may someday fly again, but you can bet your Charles Lindbergh Memorial Barf Bag it won't be a morning flight — airport bars aren't open in the morning, which I think is a big mistake. A lot of people need to relax their nerves before braving odors from unknown substances, possible blindness from laser pointers, or the things I fear most, the possibility of crashing into a mountain, lake, ocean, swamp, billboard, Winnebago, Frito's factory, Oprah Winfrey — well, you get the idea.

ABC has some explaining to do

How many of you out there watch the ABC Family Channel? The Mistress of the Manor and I watched a movie on that channel a few weeks ago and, as one might expect, the channel was promoting its other offerings during the numerous commercials. The reason I bring this up is, if ABC is promoting itself as a family channel, why in the name of Art Linkletter does every show have a lurid title. Oh, by the way, the movie we watched on the family channel was *Burlesque*. Now, I'm sure we will all agree that *Burlesque* is right up there with *Mary Poppins* and *Finding Nemo* as family fare.

After seeing an abundance of promos for shows such as "Pretty Little Liars" and "The Lying Game," I sought out the channel's web site to see what other family-friendly shows were available. I found quite a list, including "Twisted," "Switched at Birth," "Secret Life," "Baby Daddy," and "Greek."

Now, I could be wrong, but when something is advertised as being family oriented, I think that means it is appropriate for all members of the family. However, ABC apparently has other families in mind, possibly the Manson family, the Gambino family, or the Borgia family. In fact, I think it might well be the Borgias that ABC modeled their family fare on.

The Borgia family, you see, was a family prominent during the Renaissance in Italy, prominent enough to produce three

Popes. I think their names were Sodomy III, Buggerer I and Pedophile II. Anyway, they were suspected of a litany of crimes, including adultery, theft, rape, bribery, incest, and murder. They were particularly fond of poisoning their enemies with arsenic. In fact, in addition to being remembered for their corrupt rule, their name has become a synonym for treachery and poisoners.

Now, with all the talk about the problems that stem from the broken family unit, I'm a little surprised that ABC Family features shows about lying, unmarried men who father babies, and fraternities. The last time I checked, fraternities were primarily interested in two things; drinking and helping young women become unwed mothers. I don't know what the show "Twisted" is about. It could be about a serial killer who eats his victims, or Rush Limbaugh. I'm not sure. "Switched at Birth" might be about a Jewish child, reared as a Muslim, with the reversal being true for the other child. "Secret Life" lends itself to so many lurid ideas that it boggles the mind. I can think of all kinds of lurid ideas, but I don't want to give the ABC Family Channel any more ideas.

Don't get me wrong, I'm not for censorship. I don't think TV, movies, music, literature or video games makes any individual do something that they are not already predisposed to do. No TV show or any other form of entertainment is going to make someone a serial killer unless that person already has it in himself to begin with. However, I also believe in honesty in advertising.

To give you an idea of what kind of tragedy ABC's dishonesty could result in, let's look at this scenario. A mother and father are watching TV in the den, while their 12-year-old daughter is watching TV in her room. The mother decides to check on little Brittany to see if she's okay. She walks to upstairs and knocks on Brittany's door.

"Honey, what are you doing?" she asks.

"Watching TV, Mom," says Brittany.

"What program are you watching, honey?" says Mom as she walks into the room.

"It's called Pretty Little Lying Sluts Club. It's on the ABC Family Channel. You see, Chelsey is pregnant, but since she had sex with four boys on the same night, she's not sure who's the father," answers little Brittany.

Mother promptly faints, falls down the stairs and dad is left to raise little Brittany all by himself. He then begins to drink heavily, leaving little Brittany on her own. Before long little Brittany, left to her own devices and influenced by ABC programming, becomes a member of the Pretty Little Lying Sluts Club.

This tragic story could have been avoided if only ABC was more truthful. Maybe, just maybe, ABC needs to rethink the family label and go with something like the ABC Dysfunctional Channel or, at least, the ABC Wild-Ass Youth Channel.

Class reunion requires cool car

I came across an article the other day concerning high school reunions, and the changes you need to undergo to properly impress your former classmates. Now, the advice this article offered was pretty much what you would expect—lose some weight, grow some hair, have everything nipped and tucked, research very carefully the story you're going to pass off as your life, and convince the hot 18-year-old intern at your office to pretend to be your wife for the night. If she won't go for it, try a female escort, but not a cheap female escort. A cheap female escort will not provide the impression you're looking for, but might provide you with an incurable female escort disease. Those are the worst kind.

The article pointed out that the inquiring minds of your former classmates will probably ask you questions such as "Are you married?" "Where do you work?" "What do you do?" "Do you have any children in prison?" However, the writer focused the majority of the article on another question, "What kind of car do you drive?" The article then went on to list "seven cool cars for your high school reunion." A cool car is, apparently, a must for a successful high school reunion. After all, what better way to show all those people who said you would never be worth a hill of beans, worth a dime, or worth a handful of weasel mucus, just how successful you have become? They don't need to know about that 1982 Vega that has just one wiper blade, two hubcaps and three doors sitting in your garage.

Although the article put a big emphasis on the model of car one drives, I don't remember that being a topic of discussion during the last high school reunion the Mistress of the Manor and I attended, which was something like 20 years ago. Everyone sat around, talked about old times and even danced a little. Our reunion was held at what is now Carroll County Intermediate School, but was called Hillsville High School back in the long-long-ago-before time. Since alcohol is not allowed on school grounds, even for a reunion, we had to walk out to our cars to liven up our drinks, if you know what I mean, wink wink, nudge nudge. Now, this was a little inconvenient, but, at the same time, very appropriate, since we did the same thing when attending dances at the high school in our youth. Aahhh, memories — but enough of that, back to cars.

Since I appreciate nice cars, I, of course, read on to find out which cool cars would make the list. Now, I know cool cars. My youthful years, the 60s and 70s, represent the heyday of cool cars. I, myself, had a 1968 Super Sport Chevelle that was powered by a 396-cubic inch, 375-hp engine. It had white leather interior, mag wheels, dual chrome exhausts and chrome manifold covers. That baby would scoot. If I hadn't had the Chevelle, I would have gone with a GTO Judge. Of course, the highway was littered with cool, high-performance cars – Roadrunners, Camaros, Chargers, Olds

442s and Shelby Mustangs, just to name a few. In addition to being awesome driving machines, they had style. You could tell a SS Chevelle from a Roadrunner or a Camaro from a Charger with ease. Today, for the most part, all cars have pretty much the same body style. It is a Honda, or a Chevy, or a Ford? Who the heck knows without looking at the company insignia on the car?

Okay, back to the article, which said the cars on the list were selected because of their "cool appeal." It's not about being rich, necessarily, it's about being cool," so said the article. So, what names hit me smack in the face when I scrutinized the list? - Volkswagen and Hyundai, of course. Now, I don't know about you, but when I think of cool, I don't think of Hyundai. You can use many words to describe a Hyundai, but cool ain't one of them. Fuel efficient, small, inexpensive, Korean-made, but not cool.

As for the Volkswagen, I can cut it a little slack since it was cool in the long-long-ago-before time. I mean a Volkswagen van was the freak mobile of choice during those wild and wicked days of my youth. The remaining cars on the list were nice to sort of cool, but the only honest-to-God cool car was the Camaro 2SS, a true muscle car with a 426-hp engine.

Now, you're probably saying, "Why does a car have to have so much muscle to be cool? Well, for anything to be cool, it must have some danger associated with it. A headline in a London newspapers once warned parents "to lock up your daughters" when The Rolling Stones were about. A particular werewolf in

Warren Zevon's "Werewolves of London" was dangerous and a snazzy dresser as illustrated in the lines,

"You better stay away from him,

He'll rip your lungs out Jim,

Huh, I'd like to meet his tailor."

And so for a car to be cool, it must have muscle. So, when your high school reunion rolls around, leave the Subaru BRZ at home and buy or rent a restored 1968 GTO Judge. Later that night, you'll be glad you did.

Fads through the ages

It seems like every generation of young people does crazy things. In the 1920s, flagpole sitting was all the rage and in the 30s, those nutty college kids were swallowing goldfish. The 40s kids took it to a new level by fighting a war and the 50s kids thought it was cool to see how many people they could cram into a phone booth.

Now, there was one fad that started in the 40s and continued for a couple of decades. That was the panty raid. Although the first documented panty raid took place at Augastana College in Rock Island, IL, in 1948, the second didn't occur until 1952 when the men at the University of Michigan launched an assault on women's undies. That sparked a fad that ran into the 60s before petering out.

Now, of all those fads the panty raid seems like the most fun. You could fall off a flagpole and break — well, just about everything; you could choke on a goldfish and just imagine getting a cramp while stuffed like a sardine in a phone booth. But a panty raid, how much danger could there be in that? I guess you could accidentally grab a soiled pair of panties, or trip and choke yourself on a garter belt, but, really, what are the odds? In most recorded raids, all had a good time. Heck, sometimes the women cheered the men on, while throwing their unmentionables out the window.

That last bit of information reminds me of a time I locked my keys in my car after dropping the future Mistress of the Manor off at her dorm at Radford University. Realizing all I needed to break into my own car was a coat hanger, I made my way back toward the dorm. Before I got there, a couple of security guards came by and asked me ever so politely, what the hell I thought I was doing. I explained the situation to them, and they promptly told me to return to my car and stay away from the dorms. If they thought I was a longhaired degenerate stalking the young ladies, you would have thought they would have wanted me out of there, but they offered no help.

Well, I returned to my car and as soon as they got out of sight, I made my way back to the nearest dorm. The doors were locked tight so I went around the side of the building and, since there were plenty of lights on, I began to holler at the young ladies. They responded by waving, talking to me, throwing some things, including some undies; and a few even showed me things I knew the future Mistress of the Manor would not want me to look at. I can say one thing; they were healthy young ladies. Anyway, I got everything, but a coat hanger before the lights of the security guards caught my eye. I returned to my car, but instead of continuing on their route, they decided to park between the dorm and me.

Now, we're going to transition from my tangent back to the subject of fads. Some people thought rock n' roll was a fad.

We now know how wrong they were. As Neil Young sang on the "Rust Never Sleeps" album, "Hey, hey, my, my, rock n' roll will never die." However, we did have some music fads that didn't last, thank goodness. Disco, which hit a high mark in the late 70s, and an even scarier one, hair bands of the 80s come to mind. Hair bands were more about appearance than music, as evidenced by the guys teasing their long hair to outrageous extremes and wearing more makeup than a $5 hooker.

Yes, there have been many fads through the years, but today's younguns are looking to step it up a notch, at least according to an article I recently read. Among the fads are vodka-eyeballing, car surfing, drinking hand sanitizer and trunking.

As you might guess vodka-eyeballing requires pouring a shot of vodka straight into the eye. This gives you a quick buzz, but may also result in impaired vision, according to doctors. Now, I'm no doctor, although I like to play one at times, but I could figure this out on my own. Drinking hand sanitizer is equally as bad. Sanitizer contains 62 percent ethyl alcohol and if you use salt to separate the alcohol from the sanitizer, you get a 120-proof shot. A few drinks that potent and medical intervention may be needed, you know, to keep you from dying. Car surfing is just as foolish since it requires a person to stand on the roof or the trunk of a moving car. Again, death is a very real possibility.

Kids may think this trunking thing is new, something they have thought up, but, in reality, it's been around for quite a long time. You see, I participated in trunking back in the long-long-ago-before-time. Say, you're going to a drive-in. Okay, an explanation may be in order for younger readers. A drive-in is a place where they show movies on a very large screen outside and you watch the movie while seated in your car. However, in order to get more bang for your buck, one or two people ride in the car, while as many people as possible hide in the trunk, thus the term *trunking*. Again, there is danger if your trunk is rear-ended by a careless driver or if your friends, who may have been imbibing, forget about you.

Now, I'm not advocating any of these activities, past or present, but I especially caution against the newer, more dangerous fads I have mentioned. Maybe pick an oldie, but a goodie. My choice would be panty raiding. However, I need to make this clear for anyone who hasn't done this before — the young lady cannot, I repeat, cannot be in the panties when you raid them. That is called something else entirely.

How to look marvelous

Even though the weather hasn't been very good lately, we all know warm weather is a comin', it's just a matter of time. That means, of course, everybody has to get in shape. As I've said before, the only way to make the U.S. the shining star on the mount that every country in the world looks up to is for every American to look marvelous.

That means it's time to get in shape, so when you're walking along the beach, around your front yard, or through the mall in your Speedo or bikini, the out-of-shape people will drool with envy, while making a solemn vow to attain your marvelousness.

With that in mind, I've done some research and found six easy ways to speed up weight loss, so as to be just as svelte as a Cheetah. These tips come from the Lifestyle Blog at Xfinity. Hear that Xfinity people, I've just given you some free advertising! Now, do something about my way-too-high bill. Okay, back to being marvelous.

Four of the six tips for easy weight loss are right up my alley — "eat more snacks," "stop multitasking," "eat before eating" and "sleep more." In fact, I've been following most of these tips for years, especially eating more snacks and eating before eating. However, in my case that hasn't led to a more svelte body, rather to a more, let's say, mature body. Okay, okay, a slightly more portly body. Okay, stop it, a big belly. Since reading the tips, I've thought about what has gone wrong, and the only thing I can think of is I'm not eating enough snacks or not eating enough before I eat. That's the only possible answer.

Now, we all know how I feel about multitasking — it's a bad thing and can have dire consequences. Multitasking is for people who feel driven to get many things done as quickly as possible. That ain't me, Jack. I'm a firm believer in *qui vivra verra*, French for "what will be will be." The French are rude and couldn't beat a group of one-legged midgets in a war, but they do have the right attitude when it comes to the pace of life. They take lunches that last for several hours, giving them plenty of time to eat, drink wine and practice the art of love.

I also like to sleep, but I must confess I've been falling short in that category since I rejoined the world of journalism. In the previous three years before I began pounding the keys, the Mistress of the Manor and I would stay up late frolicking and casting fate to the wind. Sometimes we would not kiss the night goodbye until the wee hours of the morning. Time was on our side to paraphrase The Rolling Stones. But, alas, since becoming a working-stiff once again, my sleep time has shrunken. However, I have figured out how to solve this problem — I'm getting rid of the alarm clock.

To be honest, the other two tips for weight loss aren't exactly in my wheelhouse, so to speak. The first is to "drink more tea than water" — the reasoning being that tea is tastier than water. Now, don't get me wrong, I like me some ice tea at times, but I usually prefer water. I find it refreshing and have no problem drinking eight glasses a day. Throw in the four to five cups of black coffee a day and I'm a drinkin' a plenty. By the way, coffee is very good for a person providing at least four cups are consumed a day. Scientists say so, and I'm all about science.

The final tip on the list is definitely out, since it is "add strength training to your workout, or do more of it." It's not that I don't want to add strength training or do more of it; it's that I don't want to train at all. I figure I did enough training back in 1972 at Fort Jackson to satisfy my training quota for life. Besides, additional training will take away from the time I can spend on some of the other tips, like "eating more snacks," "eating before eating" and "sleeping more."

The God particle

I got pretty excited the other day. Not as excited as when the Mistress of the Manor agrees to play master plumber and lonely housewife, but pretty excited nonetheless. No, what got me excited the other day was the discovery of the God particle, you know, that crucial subatomic particle that could unlock the greatest mysteries of the universe.

Now, this particular particle is also known as the Higgs Boson because a nerd named Peter Higgs theorized about it in 1964. What I don't get is why the particle was named after him, considering that he didn't really find it, in reality, and isn't that what it's all about? He just suggested it existed. I have suggested, or theorized, if you will, many things over the years, just ask the Mistress of the Manor; and most of them have been rejected. Sometimes it's a simple "No." Sometimes it's an emphatic "NO!" And sometimes, it's "Are you out of your mind?"

I was the first person to theorize that if you remain in the same position for the entire basketball game your team will never lose. Okay, that theory has been proven wrong. However, it did lead to another theory, and that is, if you remain in the same position for two hours, you will need a chiropractor. That theory has been proven right. I also theorized at one time — during my distinguished college career — that if you flood your body with enough alcohol and chemicals you become the God particle. That too was proven wrong. However, it too, lead to another theory, and that is, if you flood your body with chemicals and alcohol you end up with a grade point average equal to one achieved by an off-kilter hamster.

The so-called God particle holds the critical explanation of where the mass of all matter comes from. Now, Rooster Edwards and I have both theorized on this matter. I theorized it could be found in the exhilaration of driving from Hillsville to the dorms at Radford University in just 28 minutes, while Rooster said he found it while hunting on Buffalo Mountain when he came face to face with the granddaddy of all bears, which proceeded to rip him a new one, if you know what I mean.

Anyway, once I heard the news about the discovery of the God particle I began to research the matter just to see what benefit this would have for us common folk. One source said, "We might need other models, other than the Higgs Boson, to explain the whole thing in a coherent way." Well, coherent was what I was looking for, but what I got was a bunch of double-talk and gobbledygook that led me to believe these so-called scientists weren't even sure what we had on our hands.

I finally found an article with a section entitled "How does this benefit anyone?" Now, I was expecting something like "We will now learn the meaning of life," or "We will now be able to create a utopia on the planet Earth," or "We will now be able to teleport from one place to another in a matter of seconds," or, at least, "Who put the bomp in the bomp bah bomp bah bomp, who put the ram in the rama lama ding dong." But did I find the answers to any of these pressing questions? Nnnoooooooo. Instead, I got "There is no direct benefit that we can easily see in our everyday lives."

Given this, what in the name of Enrico Fermi is all the excitement about? I mean, if we can't do fun things like teleport, or become invisible and sneak into the dressing rooms of the Victoria's Secret models, what good is this so-called God particle. Seems to me, a particle with a name like that should open up new horizons, expand our minds or, at least allow us to sneak a peek, sight unseen.

The next time scientists come out with a big announcement, claiming they've discovered something major, everybody just needs to relax. What's exciting for scientists apparently isn't what's exciting for folks of my ilk. The God particle doesn't live up to its name; maybe just call it the Rooster Edwards particle.

Magic: A wide open field for women

I don't know about you, but I love me some good magic. Yes siree, cut a woman in half, make a tiger disappear, or escape from a burning box sight unseen, and I'm a happy man. Of course, we all know there's no magic — or so the dark side would have you believe — it's all illusion. There are no magicians, there are illusionists. Nevertheless, we're going to talk about magic.

I don't know if anyone else has noticed this, but there are few women performing magic. It's always some guy in a tux or a flamenco outfit with puffy sleeves doing the magic. Of course, all his helpers are leggy beauties, but all they are good for is being cut up, disappearing or making you take your eyes off the magician. Why is that, you may ask? Well, I've given it some thought and come up with a few ideas.

The best reason, I suspect, is because they're afraid they'll be killed. We have a long history in this country of killing women who allegedly perform magic. We don't tolerate that stuff. If there's any magic to be done, the men will take care of it.

Why not long ago, I think it was in 1692, the beautiful little burg of Salem, Mass., decided it had a few too many witches. Now, a witch here or there is one thing, but when you have as many as Salem had you just have to thin the herd, and thin the herd those pious people of Salem did. According to a Robert Calef, a contemporary writer of the time, 19 women were hanged and one was "prest" to death. He did not say what was used to flatten her, but I'm guessing a bunch of rocks, or possibly a wagon. In addition, eight more women were condemned, 50 confessed to be witches and another 150 were in prison on witchcraft charges, all felonies.

Now, for the life of me, I can't understand why everybody was so upset with all the witches. I understand if the ones they killed were those green, mole-covered, hawk-nosed, piles of human waste that ate children. But, I know for a fact — okay, I surmise — that not all witches look like that. Some are hot, which makes sense. If you're a witch and can work magic, would you prefer to look like something that crawled out of Rush Limbaugh or a babe? I think most witches would go with babe.

I remember becoming intrigued; at least that's what we'll call it for the time being, with the TV show "Bewitched." Elizabeth Montgomery played Samantha, a witch who was married to a mortal. I was 14 at the time and thought what could be better; you're married to a beautiful witch; my goodness, the thoughts that raced through my hormone-filled mind. Yippee ki-yay!

Although as a young fellow I fantasized about having a beautiful witch as a wife, it turns out I was actually bewitched several years later by a fetching young beauty who eventually became the Mistress of the Manor; and, although she does have some dandy tricks, I still haven't seen her make a tiger disappear.

Although the United States and Europe both have a history of burning, hanging, drowning and pressing witches, Asia has a totally different outlook. In fact, a few hundred years ago a woman performing magic was considered high art. Their magic took the form of parlor tricks, and if there's one thing I like besides magic, its parlor tricks. Again, yippee ki-yay!

But today, the world of magic is desperately lacking when it comes to women performers, and there are some legitimate reasons, according to some female magicians. First, women's hands are smaller, making prestidigitation harder for the female gender, and then there's the clothing. Most magic tricks assume a person is wearing a jacket and pants, so as to better hide things. If you are wearing a gown — well, it's much harder to hide stuff, especially if you need to get to it quickly. Where a man might pull a rabbit out of a hat, a woman might have to pull the rabbit out of her — well, you figure it out.

There is one famous — okay, I've never heard of her either — female magician by the name of Celeste Evans, who performed in the 1960s. She did a bird act while wearing a form-fitting gown. Lisa Mena, one of the few modern female magicians, says, to this day, "Nobody has a clue where those birds came from." Hmmm, makes you wonder, doesn't it?

Then again, some people theorize that women just aren't into magic as much as men. This seems strange, since a lot of women have a long list of things they would change about their husbands if they could. Just think, women, if you learn magic, maybe you can turn someone like, say — Rooster Edwards— into someone like, say — George Clooney. Okay, that's a bit far-fetched, Merlin couldn't do that, but you get the idea.

So, I say, women, become magicians! Make tigers disappear, cut men in half, pull bunnies out of hidden places and by all means do parlor tricks. Yippe ki-yay!

Virginia aiming for greatness

Everyone knows that Virginia abounds in history. Our beloved state is known as the "Mother State" because we were the first state colonized. Virginia is also known as the "Mother of Presidents," because eight men who became our nation's supreme leader were born on this hallowed ground.

Before I go any further, I need to address a false claim by Ohio, which, apparently, will lay claim to just about anything, except the Cleveland Browns. Ohio claims to be the birthplace of flight because the Wright brothers were born in that state, choosing to forget the fact they chose North Carolina as the place to make history. While I find that annoying, the false claim that gets my goat, burns my bacon, scorches my chicken is the state's claim to — wait for it — being the "Birthplace of Presidents," Yea, that's right those buckeye bozos are trying to undercut the Old Dominion.

Ohio claims to have birthed eight future presidents, while claiming that Virginia has produced just seven. A little research has straightened out this discrepancy. Those buckeyes claim William Henry Harrison, our ninth president. However, records show Harrison didn't live in Ohio until after he was married in 1795. He was born at Berkeley Plantation in Charles City County, Virginia. So there buckeyes, suck on that.

Now, let's move on to a question I have about Old Virginnie. What has happened to our once great state? Many Virginians were key players in the founding of this nation and three of the first six presidents were homegrown. But since Woodrow Wilson, who was president from 1913-1921, we've been, for the most part, a non-player on the national scene. Before I go any further, I need to set the record straight. When I was in high school, students learned Wilson was a great president. I learned later, he was a racist and we had more foreign interventions (nine) under him than any president in our history. I'm sure Eric Cantor still admires him, though.

So, with Virginia falling off the face of the presidential map, it's only natural that we need something to catch the eye of our fellow states. Well, my friends, our lawmakers are doing their best to bring us back to the forefront. I'm sure everybody knows our legislators are much more concerned with women's reproductive organs than they are getting automatic weapons off the streets. Yep, those darn vaginas are the problems, not weapons designed for killing as many people in the shortest amount of time as possible.

On top of that, a proposal to study whether Virginia should adopt its own currency is apparently gaining support in the state legislature. One supporter is Republican Del. Robert Marshall, who wants a 10-member panel appointed to study this matter. Marshall wants a return to the gold standard, which was suspended in 1933 by Franklin Roosevelt. By the way, Fort Knox is empty, according to the History Channel. It must be remembered though that the History Channel also televised a program raising the question, "Did space aliens attend the first Thanksgiving?" Oh, by the way, the answer is "yes."

Now, if Virginia decides to print its own money, backed by actual gold, our government will need a lot of the shiny stuff, and a place to keep it. I've already decided to offer storage space in my basement, free of charge. In addition, we need to decide who should be on our currency. Marshall has already ruled out Jefferson Davis and Dave Matthews, and since Washington and Jefferson are already on coins, they are, in my opinion, right out. However, that still leaves a wide-open field of famous Virginians who could adorn state currency.

I think it would be only fair to allow our citizenry to have a say so as to who will be pictured on our money. In addition to the other U.S. presidents born in Virginia, I'm sure Confederate heroes like Robert E. Lee, Stonewall Jackson and Jeb Stuart would get mention, or possibly famous actors like Warren Beatty, George C. Scott and Shirley MacLaine — okay, nobody's going to want crazy Shirley on their money — or authors like Tom Wolfe and Willa Cather.

However, I think we need to think outside the box. If we're going to tell the rest of the U.S. we don't need your stinkin' money, well, I think we need to go in another direction.

Personally, I am voting for Nat Turner, Bill "Bojangles" Robinson and Pocahontas. Turner, of course, led a great slave uprising, Mr. Bojangles could really dance around (almost as good as our current politicians dance around the real issues) and Pocahontas was a Native-American who got it on with a white man. I think they are perfect representatives of our great Commonwealth.

We don't need no learnin'

I'm a lover of books and so is the Mistress of the Manor. We read virtually every day, a lot of the time to each other. Our humble manor and garage are cluttered with books, massive amounts of books. Although the majority of the books are fiction, we have plenty of books dealing with history, religion, politics, and, of course, aliens and zombies. The only kinds of books we don't have are those of the self-help or self-improvement variety. Why? Because we don't need no stinkin' help or improvement, we are fine just the way we are.

As you might expect, when I saw a list about the most and least literate cities in these great United States my interest was aroused. Where do the erudite dwell? Where do the refined reside? Where do the well-versed lodge? Then I thought, who cares, I want to know which squalid cities house the people who think a Chlamydia brochure is literature. Well, it appears that the majority live in California and Texas. Really, is this any surprise? Hell, in Texas a completed coloring book is considered fine art.

Cities were judged on the weekly newspaper circulation, the percentage of adults with a college degree and the number of retail bookstores per 10,000 people. Now, the newspaper and bookstore categories I feel are legitimate measure of literacy, however, I'm not so sure about the college degree category. You see, I attended college and even graduated, much to the surprise of my parents, who thought I was planning to make college attendance a vocation. During my illustrious college career, and yes, it was illustrious; I knew a lot of very smart people. I also knew people who would go on to graduate despite soaking up about as much knowledge as a pitted prune. There are plenty of people working for minimum wage, participating in illegal activities and sleeping in a van down by the river, who are much smarter than many with college degrees. The mind, not the certificate, determines intelligence.

Anyway, back to the squalid cities of which I spoke earlier. California is the runaway winner in the least-literate category with five, yes, count them, five cities on the 10-city list. This is not surprising since the U.S. Department of Education ranks the state dead last with a 23-percent illiteracy rate. Bakersfield claimed the top spot, which would make Buck Owens very proud if he wasn't dead. The city ranks third from the bottom in both the number of booksellers and periodicals such as newspapers and journals, but, on the bright side, is the nation's leader in underarm odor. Stockton was third, Anaheim fifth, Fresno seventh and Long Beach 10th. Apparently, books and newspapers have been outlawed in most areas of the state, so most Californians rely on liquor bottles and jars of Cheez Whiz for reading material.

Texas is represented on the list by three cities — runner-up Corpus Christi, No. 4 El Paso and No. 6 San Antonio. Since the main source of reading material for Texans is the brands that appear on cattle's butts, it's not surprisingly the Lone Star State ranks 47th in illiteracy with a 19 percent rate. Texans are, however, number one in armadillo molestations. It should also be noted that Corpus Christi's library resources were among the worst in the nation, mainly because none of the books had been completely colored.

Now, you probably noticed there are two states in between Texas and California at the bottom of the literacy rankings. Those two proud states are Florida, 20 percent illiteracy rate, and New York, 22 percent. And while that is an important fact to know if you're thinking of relocating, the bigger question may be how did Virginia fare? Well, not so well. The Old Dominion has an illiteracy rate of 12 percent, tying it with Kentucky and Oklahoma for 29th. So to all my fellow Virginians, if books aren't for you, please, please, please don't rely on a Cheez Whiz jar for your reading material, lift up your standards. I hear the Grey Poupon label is excellent reading.

All good things come to an end

We have recently added a new member to our household, a creature both alien and familiar. At first, I didn't think we could get along, but time has somewhat warmed my feelings for this creature. Although, like this morning when it decided to take a sip of my coffee while my back was turned, I have the urge to impale it with a sharp object. What creature can cause one to respond with kindness one moment and blind hatred the next? Why, it's a cat, of course.

Now, the Mistress of the Manor and I didn't go looking for a cat. If I were looking for a pet, it would be a dog. Dogs provide unconditional love, while cats only cozy up to you when they want something. The rest of the time, they wouldn't care if you were on fire.

Our cat, that term still gives me chills, was apparently a well-cared-for feline (she had been fixed) until its owners decided to move without telling it to pack its bags. It ended up with our neighbor, who was expecting a new arrival of her own — a Great Dane puppy — in a few days, so she asked if we wanted the cat. Oddly enough, the Mistress of the Manor seemed inclined to the idea, but once our neighbor brought the subject up in front of our grandson — well, we had to take the cat. Wild Man quickly decided on Maple Leaf for its name and it begrudgingly joined our household.

Now, pets are nothing new to me. Growing up, we had two dogs – a loving, sweet, collie named Jack, and a terrier-Chihuahua mix named Cookie with the temperament of Rush Limbaugh on crack. Just ask her veterinarian. He's dead now, and I'm still not sure she didn't have something to do with it. Jack would sit quietly while the vet vaccinated him, but when it became Cookie's turn, that little bit of hell went berserk. She destroyed more than one muzzle, as well as a few fingers. She developed cancer, and her passing was a blessing — for everyone concerned. The vet even sent a congratulations card.

I was also very familiar with cats by this time, since my sister had somewhere in the vicinity of a million, or, at least, it seemed that way. Of course, one winter we cut that number down to size, and I mean that literally. It seemed the cats and kittens alike found they could keep warm by crawling up onto the motors of our cars at night. The first time this happened, it resulted in fillet of kitty the next morning. Although we tried to check each morning, sometimes we forgot. And when we forgot, another kitty or two went to that great scratching post in the sky.

My all-time favorite pet was a German shepherd-collie mix named Booger. I got him from one of my drama professors while at college. We bonded the first night I had him when he crawled into bed with me. As I was dozing off, I felt Booger step up onto my chest. I then felt a warm sensation, followed by a wet sensation. Booger had peed on me.

Despite his eventual 120-some pounds, Booger proved over the years to be a gentle creature, except when it came to skunks. That dog sought out skunks, which was a bad thing in more ways than one. Not only did he return from his skunk hunting smelling to high Heaven, his face would be swollen to the size of a basketball. The vet said Booger was allergic to skunks, but, to his credit, Booger never flinched from his mission of destroying all the smelly creatures he could.

While my kids were growing up, we had dogs and cats galore. My daughter had, at one time, cats in the double-digits, and, although we never had that many dogs at one time, we had more than enough. One dog in particular, Boogie, was as dumb as a bag of hammers. Others were smart, some were noisy and some hated cats. As our kids got older, our number of pets slowly diminished, until we didn't have any. And that was fine, because we were petted out. At least as far as animals were concerned.

My daughter, or "Dammit" as she was known during one exhausting Christmas shopping trip (her brother was known as "Hell Fire" at that time) loved the cats as a youngun', but is now totally a dog person. Her beloved Gilbert, who looks like a miniature German shepherd, was a bit neurotic for a portion of his life, and would bark at the Mistress of the Manor and me, and would not let us pet him unless Bernadette (her real name) or Eric (her husband) were standing next to him. That only lasted eight years. Gilbert is now cool with us, I think because we make sure we have a healthy supply of bologna on hand when he comes to visit.

Although we love Gilbert, we hadn't felt the need for another pet for the past 12 years or so. But as they say, all good things must come to an end. We now have Maple Leaf, who was on shaky ground the first couple of weeks. For some reason, she would sleep about 20 hours a day and then rouse up about 5 a.m. in the morning. Since she was up and ready for action, I guess she figured we should be up too, so she would jump into our bed and began rubbing against our heads and start meowing like she was auditioning for a *Pet Sematary* remake. It was rather disconcerting, not to mention downright annoying.

She seems to have calmed down over the past couple of weeks, and now acts more normal, which is a good thing. I actually have begun to develop warmness toward her. However, don't get me wrong. Any more of that devil cat stuff and her furry butt is in a heap of trouble.

How we won our independence from France

Belief is a funny thing. Some people believe Big Foot exists, others don't; some people believe we are being visited by aliens, others don't; some people believe the Kardashians are the spawn of Satan, others say the spawn of Big Foot.

Yes, we are raised to believe in a lot of things — Santa Claus, the Easter Bunny, the Tooth Fairy and, in my case, Mr. Galoshes. Now, you may not be familiar with Mr. Galoshes, but let me tell you, don't dare cross him. It's easy to believe in almost anything when you're a child. Let's face it, your brain is pretty much the same consistency as the inside of a peach, making it real easy for adults to make up stories about a man who wears only galoshes and punishes children when they misbehave.

However, when you become an adult, or at least an adult age, you should be a better judge of what is real and what is not. This is not always the case, though, as evidenced by an article on a web site entitled "Ten Weird Things" people actually believe. Mr. Galoshes didn't make the list. I'm not sure where the home base of the web site is, but all the figures are results of polls conducted in the U.S. and Britain. While Americans come off badly, the British really look stupid. But, hey, they can't help it. They didn't discover dentistry until 1987.

One thing that was startling, almost as much as Mr. Galoshes was that in a poll of British youths, 40 percent couldn't figure out the link between a cow and milk, or a chicken and an egg. In fact, 11 percent thought eggs and milk came from wheat. Yeah, from wheat! Now, if you think about the great minds that Britain spawned — Sir Isaac Newton, Sir Francis Bacon, Benny Hill — you have to wonder just when did things begin to go south in the old country. I'm not sure, but I think it had something to do with Prince Charles and that other guy, Camilla Parker Bowles.

But amazing stupidity is not limited to the British youth, ooh no, adults also appear to be missing a crumpet or two. Now, everyone knows fruit is good for you. The fact that there is more to fruit than just its color is apparently lost on 10 percent of British parents, who thought items such as orange-flavored cake, fruit-flavored candy, and, this is the best one, Coca-Cola could be counted as a portion of fruit. To top it off, one in 20 people didn't realize an orange was a fruit. With that in mind, it's not surprising that dentists make a fortune in Britain.

Now, one more thing and I'll leave the British alone. You remember, I mentioned Newton earlier, the guy who more or less discovered gravity. Well, 18 percent of the British think they can see gravity. Yes, they think they know what gravity looks like. The article didn't describe what these people thought gravity looked like, but I'm guessing it sort of looks like Mr. Galoshes. Wait a minute. I lied. I'm not finished with the British. Over a fifth of the Britains believe that light sabers exist, 24 percent believe humans can be teleported and a whopping 40 percent believe that hover boards exist. And you thought Monty Python was silly.

Now, let's turn to the good old USA, and talk about Independence Day. You know, the day we celebrate our freedom from France. Yes, yes, yes, I know, you thought it was Britain. Well, you are right, but, when asked, only 76 percent of Americans correctly identified Britain as our former ruler. Nineteen percent of those responding weren't sure which country we fought for our independence and two percent were damn sure it was France. Obviously, if we had fought France in our war of independence, we would have won our freedom much earlier, somewhere around 1710. The poor French, they are not good at la fighting. Germany can vouch for that. Another three percent of astute patriots selected countries such as Russia, China and Mexico as American's former rulers.

As for the moon landing, six percent of Americans and 25 percent of the British believe it was faked. Yes, it was all smoke and mirrors, bassoons and harmonicas, plastic wrap and oatmeal. Now, Rooster Edwards is one of many who believe the moon landing was faked. Of course, Rooster also believes that Wilford Brimley is the most interesting man on earth and that Jodie Foster is straight. And since we're dealing with space, let me throw this out for consideration. In another poll, 18 percent of Americans thought the sun revolves around the earth, while another three percent didn't know that the earth revolves around the sun.

We'll get back to the young people for this closing bit of absurdity. A couple of years ago when the 100th anniversary of the sinking of the Titanic was making the news, many young people got confused. Twitter was alive with tweets from teens and young adults who were surprised to find out that the story of the Titanic was real, not just a movie. This is troublesome on many levels and makes us wonder about our future.

Heck, in another 50 years, when asked how World War II started, you might get something like this, "Well, the vampires, led by Edward the Great, were traveling on a ship named the Titanic when a werewolf submarine, captained by Jacob the Hairy, sank it, causing every country in the world to declare war against one another. The world was saved, however, when a great wizard named Harry Potter defeated France all by himself. Potter then created a paradise on earth. Egg and milk trees grew in abundance, and there was plenty of healthy orange cake for everyone."

Shortly after that explanation, God brings the hammer down and starts all over again.

I spit on the Grammys

I watched the Grammys a few weeks ago, not because I was anxious see all my favorite performers, rather to see which no-talent piles of mucus would be treated as if they had performed an opus that would stand the test of time. They were in abundance, the no-talent piles of mucus, that is.

Apparently, the voters who award the Grammys are a tone-death, oatmeal-for-brains, creativity-hating bunch of moneychangers who look at one thing — sales. Real talent does get nominated at times, but 99.99 percent of the time, the most inane, common, piece of garbage wins. Now, you may say, "Dear sir, could you please present some samples of the Grammys' shortcomings?" And I would say, "You bet your Stratocaster I can!" Sorry for yelling.

Okay, let's look at the biggest winners in Grammy history. The top dog, the big cheese, the wunderkind of the wand is Sir Georg Solti, who won 31 of the buggers. Now, Georg won all his for classical music, which I appreciate once every six years. It's a personal rule. So, forget the classical music category because homey don't play that game.

High on the list of all-time Grammy winners are U2 with 22 awards, Kanye West with 21, and Jay Z and Beyonce with 17 apiece. Then we have newcomers like John Legend who has won nine Grammys since 2005 and Taylor Swift who has won seven since 2009. Incredible. Swift writes a song about dropping ice cream on her favorite dress and the Grammys bestow an award on her, while Beyonce wins, I can only assume, because she's attractive and is willing to show off her best assets. Those assets are not talent, by the way.

The Grammys have chosen to honor deserving talent, after all Stevie Wonder has won 22 awards, Bruce Springsteen has won 20, Aretha Franklin has won 18, Eric Clapton and Ray Charles 17 each and B.B. King has won 15. These totals may sound good, but there are misleading. Did Clapton, as leader of Derek and the Dominos, win for "Layla" in 1972? No, he won for "Tears in Heaven" in 1990. And how about the three great bands — The Yardbirds, Cream and Blind Faith — that are part of Clapton's legacy? Did they win any Grammys? No. Quick quiz, what two other guitar greats played with The Yardbirds?

On to Springsteen, whose 1975 release "Born to Run" is one of the greatest albums in the history of rock music. "Born to Run," "Thunder Road" and "Jungleland" are tributes to not only great music but also great lyrics. In 1982, Springsteen released "Nebraska," a dark album that deals with the challenges of ordinary, blue-collar people facing difficult times. Although some of his previous albums had offered some salvation, there is none in "Nebraska," which is a bleak, but beautifully written masterpiece. Of course, Springsteen didn't win a Grammy until 1984.

Before I unleash my final tirade, let me just give you a short list of groups who have never won a Grammy — Led Zeppelin, Janis Joplin, Jimi Hendrix, The Who, Credence Clearwater Revival, The Animals, The Band, The Kinks, The Doors, The Byrds and Queen. Yet, Michael Bolton has won two and Madonna seven. Methinks bozos abound.

Now, I don't have time to list every injustice inflicted by the Grammy people, so I'll just turn to the three that really, really get me steamed. Neil Young and The Rolling Stones have each won — get ready for it, one Grammy apiece. Young won in 2010 and The Stones in 1995.

Young is a brilliant songwriter, weaving imagery with intelligent lyrics on the personal side of life, as well as leveling justified criticism of our government's shortcomings. Although Young's lyrics are the bedrock for his status as one of rock's greatest, he can blow the roof off when he wants to. I put Young and Springsteen neck-and-neck as music's second-best lyricists. You shouldn't even have to ask who number one is.

Despite receiving eight Grammys, my all-time favorite performer has been shortchanged. Bob Dylan, who is without a doubt the greatest lyricist who has ever penned a song, has changed music more than any other artist, starting with his protest music of the 1960s. He has since explored virtually every type of musical genre during his five-decade career. The Grammys finally gave Dylan his first award in 1979 for "Gotta Serve

Somebody." It took 15 years for him to get another one. However, during a time when Dylan's music was changing a nation, enlightening the minds of young people and bringing to light the malfeasance of our government, the Grammys ignored him. No Grammy for "Blowin' In the Wind," no Grammy for "Masters of War," no Grammy for "The Times They Are a-Changin'," no Grammy for "Like A Rolling Stone," no Grammy for "Desolation Row." As far as I'm concerned, Dylan should have at least 50 Grammys by now.

What can I say about The Rolling Stones, the world's greatest rock n' roll band? The Stones put together a run of excellence from 1968 to 1972 with "Beggars Banquet," "Let It Bleed," "Sticky Fingers" and "Exile on Main St." which will never be matched. Although there have been a few misses during The Stones' 50-year run, they still sell out arenas, still out-rock 20 year olds and still influence legions of young musicians to aspire to be the best. No rocker has ever matched the stage presence of Mick Jagger and no guitar player can out-riff Keith Richards. The Glimmer Twins turn 70 this year, but considering Jagger's penchant for staying in shape and Richards' apparently immunity to all drugs and diseases, they could be rockin' for another 20 years. Hell, they might even win a second Grammy.

Now, I know some younger readers may think I'm an old fart who never listens to any music that doesn't fit into the classic rock category. True, most of my listening and viewing pleasure comes from that era. But I also enjoy hearing new groups who show the creativity that most music today lacks. Old Crow Medicine Show, The Lumineers, Alabama Shakes and a genius named Jack White are all outstanding. And there's nary a 40-year-old, much less a 60-year-old, among them. I have yet to see Alabama Shakes or Jack White in concert, but I have seen the other two, and they are well worth it. In fact, The Lumineers and Alabama Shakes were each nominated for an award in the recent Grammys. They didn't win, but, who knows, in another 20 years the Grammys might finally recognize their talent.

Is it the end of the world yet?

Okay, so far, so good. It's 1:30 p.m. on Friday, the infamous Dec. 21, 2012, as I write this, and, so far, no huge fireballs, no giant cracks in the earth, and, most importantly, no zombies. Now, there's still plenty of time for the bottom to drop out of this mortal coil, but if you're reading this, more than likely the world has survived. Either that or I have a bigger fan base in the zombie community than I thought I did.

You're probably wondering, "What do I do with the stockpile of canned spinach in my basement?" "Will the finance company take a couple of AK-47s as a car payment?" "Can I somehow take a deduction on my income taxes for that bunker I built in the backyard?" Well, I'm no expert, although I pretend to be at times, but I'm going to say, "No." However, there are some things you should do if this old world is still turning, according to the experts. I'll give you a heads-up, I'm ignoring just about all of them. I take that back, I'm ignoring all of them.

The first thing you should do, according to the experts, is "review your credit history" and the second is "check out your tax situation." Neither of these sounds very appealing. My credit history is not something I want to revisit and my tax situation depends on whether President Obama or the King of Orange, John Boehner, has the best poker face.

The third thing on the list, "clear clutter," is not new advice to me. No, siree, the Mistress of the Manor addresses my clutter on a routine basis. You see, she likes things neat, whereas I can clutter with the best of them. It's not that I clutter intentionally, it's just that I find so many things essential to my sense of well-being, whether it be a Bob Dylan T-shirt that is now completely in shreds or a "Rolling Stone" magazine from 1972. I need these things.

Ranking number four on the list is a "plan for disaster," and we're not talking about the zombie or giant meteor kind of disaster. No, we're talking about doing a home inventory of your belongings, which is tough when you have clutter, and making sure, you have enough insurance, but aren't paying too much for it. This, like pretty much all the things on the list, is something any responsible adult should do — responsible, being the key word. That, of course, gives me a way out.

The next five things on the list are "review investments," "support a charity," "max out retirement contributions," "spend your flexible spending account," and "prepay bills." The experts say you can review your investments in "under an hour," heck, I can review mine in a matter of seconds. I do support charities, but as for the rest, especially "prepay bills," those just pipe dreams. There's a due date on a bill for a good reason.

The next two suggestions from the experts are "find a financial advisor" and "tinker with your budget." No financial advisor in his right mind would take me on as a client. A financial advisor and I could tinker until the cows come home, whatever that means, and we still couldn't afford one spray tan.

Another expert suggestion is "change your passwords." Now, of all the advice given thus far, this has to be the most ridiculous one of the bunch. Hell, I can barely remember my present passwords. I've tried to heed the advice of experts who say, "Don't use the same password more than once." What has that gotten me? Heartache, nothing but heartache. Sometimes, I run out of chances before I can login to a particular page, and have to try numerous times before unlocking my secret code. Is the password for this page *Howl7624/upyours* or *helpmegod3#*? I don't know!

Now, if you've decided to take the advice of these experts, you may be scratching your head, or possibly another part of your anatomy, and asking, "Just how long will this take?" These so-called experts claim that all but one of these tasks can be completed with just 13 to 18 hours of effort, while another one could take between one hour and a month. That last one is right out. I'm not spending a month on anything.

The key, they say, is taking it slow, easy, and gradual. They say earmark just 15 minutes to an hour per day and go down the list. Heck, you can even do a lot of it while watching TV, they say. Well, trying to be a responsible adult and watch TV at the same time is multi-tasking, and I think all of you know how I feel about that. I realize they think they're helping, but that flag ain't getting saluted no matter how many times they run it up the flag pole. No, siree, I didn't survive the zombie apocalypse, only to kill myself being a responsible adult.

Fall a great time for me

There are a lot of things the Mistress of the Manor and I find equally satisfying. We both love music, we both love literature, we both love movies, we both love playing stranger-at-the-door; however, there is one thing we don't agree on. Well, there are actually several things we don't agree on, which are due, in part, to her being left-handed and doing things wrong — sorry, backwards — okay, differently. I hate it when she sneaks up on me. Of course, there are things we disagree on that don't revolve around her affliction, like the importance of cable, where to put dirty clothes and Rod Stewart. Okay, I know Rod has gotten a little, okay, very cheesy in his old age, but in his youth, he and Faces were mighty fine.

There is another disagreement, and this one is lengthy and on-going. Depending on whether the Mayans were eating mushrooms or not when they came up with their now infamous calendar, this difference of opinion will last until at least Dec. 21, 2012, and possibly to May of 2013. This disagreement is over sports, specifically college football and basketball. I love sports and the Mistress of the Manor thinks they are a complete waste of time, which, of course, is absurd.

Although my love of sports has been a part of me since I was a wee child, it intensified 10 fold when one Saturday afternoon I sat down to watch some TV after mowing the yard.

Since cable or satellite dishes were a thing of the future in 1964, college football or basketball games were rarely seen on TV. However, this was not just any ordinary day, no siree. As I turned the channel knob — life was tough when I was a young spit — I came across a basketball game and immediately became intrigued. There was a white guy who could jump out of the gym. No, really, he was a white guy who could really jump. His name was Billy Cunningham, otherwise known as The Kangaroo Kid, and he played for the University of North Carolina. From that point on I was an avid Tar Heels follower. Three years later, after I had traveled to Blue Heaven to see the Tar Heels play in person, avid turned into fanatic. Although it was basketball that got me hooked on the Tar Heels, soon I was also dedicated to the football team.

Now, the Mistress of the Manor knew this in our courting days, so my addiction to anything dealing with Carolina was well known to her before we tied the knot 40 wonderful years ago. I think she hoped my interest in Carolina Blue would fade; but, bless her heart, it has only grown stronger with time.

Although she, at times, joins in my celebrations of the Tar Heels' successes, even these times get her on edge, because she is afraid I'm going to have a heart attack because of my intensity when watching Carolina play. It should be pointed out, however, that I am more easy-going about losses than I used to be. I've mellowed with age, although a certain rat-faced coach can still send me into a tirade.

In the long-long-ago-before-time, there was one time I punched a hole in the wall of our apartment after a Carolina loss in NCAA regional play. Thankfully, the Mistress of the Manor had already taken Dirty Dog Engineer, the name my small son preferred to be called at that time, out of the room. Of course, there was plenty of throwing things and cursing and other unseemly behavior.

Although I now remain relatively calm during a loss, one thing hasn't changed – superstitions or quirks, if you will. Both the Mistress of the Manor and I used to smoke. Prior to the start of the game, I would place my drink and ashtray in easy reaching distance. Now, at no time during the game, even halftime, were these two things to be moved from their appointed positions. At times, the Mistress of the Manor would pick up the ashtray in order to place it in a convenient spot for each of us, which, of course, drew a stern reprimand. In addition, I always wear Carolina gear while watching a game. If the Tar Heels lose, that shirt is retired and will not make a game appearance until next season. Believe me; I am not short on Carolina attire.

One superstition that has been altered slightly, however, deals with food. In the past, while a game was in contention, I would not eat, not even during halftime, which frustrated the Mistress of the Manor, who had slaved in a hot kitchen for my benefit. I have since altered that superstition, so that I now eat during timeouts and halftime, so far, so good.

The part of the football and basketball seasons that frustrates the Mistress of the Manor, the most is scheduling problems that arise. You see, I hate to miss a televised game, so plans involving other people and other events often have to be changed in order to accommodate my Carolina fix. It is at these times I think the Mistress of the Manor is going to punch a wall, or, possibly, me.

Happy Birthday, Little Wyatt Earp

Looking for a cool place to have your eight-year-old's next birthday party? Say you're tired of battling rabid squirrels in the park, overly aggressive geeks in the arcade or the creepiness of Zotch the half-drunk clown? You just want something new? Something that will tickle that little booger so much that he or she won't ask you for so much as a quarter for a couple of days?

Well, I found it. It's a novel idea, somewhat off the beaten track as far as birthday parties go, but one that promises lots of fun and excitement — especially excitement. The one drawback is that this unique way to celebrate the birthday of Little Biff has not yet caught on in Virginia. However, if you've got the time and money for a trip to the Texas, well, you can treat your child to a birthday he or she is sure to get a bang out of. I'm talking about holding Little Brittany's birthday at a gun range. Yes, you read that correctly — a gun range. Leave it to Texas, always a pioneer in progressive new ideas, to come up with something like this.

Now, Little Rodney has to be at least eight years old. I mean you can't go putting a gun in the hands of just any little kid. As David Prince, owner of the Eagle Gun Range, says, "You have to be tall enough to get above the shooting table." Safety first has always been Dave's mantra.

Dave promises these eight-year-olds full of awe and wonder won't be allowed to just blast away without any precautions. No siree, these little Wyatt Earps and Annie Oakleys will be supervised, either by parents or the gun range's crack crew of safety officers — Ed "Three Toes" Hickok, Bob "One Eye" Cody and, of course, Festus "The Gelding" Masterson.

According to someone, I think it's Dave; this idea has been well received by the citizens of Lewisville. It should be noted that the population of Lewisville is 60 percent brain dead, 35 percent homicidal maniacs and five percent well adjusted, reasonable people. Oh, and there is one Mormon. One of the normal people, her name is Dawn, says, "It makes me nervous. I think eight-year-olds, developmentally, can't tell the difference between play and reality sometimes." She adds that handing over weapons to eight-year-olds in "a party or game atmosphere" only heightens the chance that Little Thumbelina is going to get her ear shot off.

But as I noted before, Dave is well aware of the dangers. That's why he's introducing partying eight-year-olds to loaded guns. He's educating these budding sharpshooters on gun safety. Until Dave mentioned gun safety, I was a little worried. I mean, if we teach Little Timmy to safely shoot the eye out of a deer at a hundred yards, won't this world be a better place? I know I'll feel safer knowing that any eight-year-old toddling down the street is capable of putting a bullet between my eyes at 20 paces.

Now, even though Dave is the first gun-range owner to come up with the birthday party idea, he is not the first to see the almost obvious link between loaded weapons and eight-year-olds.

Last November, a gun club in Arizona got the exceptionally bright idea of hosting a Christmas Day photo shoot (oh yes, the pun is intended). Imagine the proud parents when they showed the picture of Little Ellen in Santa Claus' lap, holding a semiautomatic weapon. Geez, it brings tears of joy to your eyes. It also brought pain to Santa's bowels when Little Fred accidently discharged a round into the Old Geezer.

Now, some of you are probably saying, who does this namby-pamby, old-hippie bozo think he is? Some may be even more descriptive. Well, I admit people of my ilk (peace and love, man) have been in decline since the long-long-ago-before time of my youth. I must also admit a dark secret – I am a trained killer.

Yes, I know it's hard to believe, but back in 1972, the government sent an envoy to secure my services for the defense of this great country. Okay, that's not really, what happened. I actually received a letter saying I was being drafted. Anyway, the only part of basic training I enjoyed was shooting the various weapons the instructors regretfully placed into our hands. Since most of us were draftees, they weren't sure handing loaded weapons to us was a good idea. You can build up a lot of resentment running five miles in full pack in the 100-degree heat of Columbia, S.C.

Anyway, the point is, I loved the weapons, so I can see how an eight-year-old can get hooked. Since eight-year-olds are basically silly little creatures, gunplay could easily result in accidental wounding — the more kids, the more wounding. But once they hit the teen years, look out, the stakes get much higher.

Now, maybe I'm just being a little negative. Maybe there is a bright side to a gun-range birthday party. Maybe when we die, we jet into outer space and become a god of our own planet. But maybe I'm right. You know, kids change a lot between the ages of eight and, say, 15, when they become moody, antagonistic and, generally, a pain in the butt. That innocent little eight-year-old who might accidentally shoot you in the kidney becomes a teenager who decides to go for a high body count at Wal-Mart.

Tackiness knows no bounds at Christmas

If you're like me — okay, okay, I didn't mean to insult you — you are still decorating for Christmas. Why? Because you can never be too tacky when celebrating the birth of Baby Jesus. Now, Jesus didn't go in for a lot of frills, he was more concerned with feeding the hungry, healing the sick and being a thorn in the side of the establishment. However, in today's world we chose to honor him with dancing reindeer, smiling snowmen and elves of suspect gender.

Although the Mistress of the Manor and I keep our inside decorations tasteful and refined, when it comes to the outside of the manor, we attempt to be as tacky as everyone else is. Our outside decorations this Christmas season — that's right, Christmas season, not holiday season — began with an unexpected adornment — our normal inside tree. After retrieving the tree from our outbuilding, we proceeded to decorate like a couple of elves high on Santa sugar. When we were done, the tree was absolutely beautiful.

However, we soon noticed a strange odor in our beloved abode. What was it? Well, anytime there's a strange odor in the house, the Mistress of the Manor immediately claims there's a dead mouse behind the refrigerator. Why it's always the refrigerator, I don't know. Possibly, because when a mouse knows it's dying, its natural instincts tell it to seek solace behind the hardest to move object in a house, or the Mistress of the Manor likes to see the veins pop out on my forehead. It could be either. Anyway, the smell became rather unpleasant, something akin to a dead mouse (not my words) or the afterbirth of an elf-reindeer hybrid.

We began narrowing the possibilities after looking behind every object in the house (I found no dead mice), and soon realized it was our most beautiful Christmas tree that was releasing the pungent odor. It had been stored in the same plastic box that it has been stored in for 10 years or so, so why it decided to start stinking things up is anybody's guess. It could have something to do with mice, refrigerators or gender-challenged elves, I just don't know. So, we dragged it outside to our front porch, ornaments and all, and there it still resides. We did move the ornaments to our new inside tree, but left the lights on the old, stinky tree to add a festive spirit to the porch.

However, that wasn't enough. We then added garland to the porch railings, as well as red ribbon to produce a candy cane effect. To emphasize that theme, we hung giant candy canes from the railing. Oh yes, we have two deer that light up, wreaths on the front and back, and there may be more to come. Now, we're not trying to go for any record here. I mean there are homesteads in this little burg that make us look like a one-bulb wonder. Now, whether you have enough decorations to create an electric bill that surpasses that of Bangladesh or a small amount like me, they have one thing in common. All decorations look much better after dark.

Yes, at night, all those pretty lights look so beautiful, so dazzling. The more lights you have, the bigger the bang. However, when the sun rises, it's a different story. The less decoration of the lighted variety you have, the better off you are. While the front of our home may look like someone spilled a box of lights and giant candy canes on our porch, some homes look like Christmas drank way too much spiked eggnog and threw up on them. Those lighted reindeer look great at night, but in the light of day, they resemble assembled skeletons. Those lights that encircle the house, lighting it up like a magical castle at night, scream Kentucky in July during the bright sun.

Therein lies the conundrum. Is the beauty of the night worth the tackiness of the day? Are the high electric bills and long hours of physical labor worth the *oohs* and *aahs* of passersby? Is the elf that Santa was spotted with at Club Naughty really his niece? So many questions; so few answers. However, when in doubt, don't spare the juice. Light it up, and light it up big. Tackiness is as much a part of Christmas as belligerent relatives who drink too much, gaudy sweaters that scream, "Shoot me, now!" and, yes, stinky Christmas trees.

First date advice

Aaahhh, first dates, they are the things of legend. Now, I'm not talking about the first date with your beloved, unless, of course, your beloved is the only person you ever dated, no, no, no. I'm certainly not talking about the very first time you picked up "Crazy Marie" at the Bunker & Bullets Bar. No, I'm talking about the very first time you got spiffed up, drove to the home of a young lady you barely knew and took her to a movie, or dancing, or some dark spot off the highway.

Those first dates can be charming, magical, and delightful. They can be — but, more often than not, they are horror stories that still make you cringe years later. Now, this may be truer for people of my generation than the present generation, I don't know. I wanted to find out about the dating habits of the present generation, but the Mistress of the Manor said that my dating 18-year-olds was right out.

The reason I'm writing about dating is due to an article I read that was entitled "Don't say this on a first date." Strangely enough, just the other day the Mistress of the Manor and I were reminiscing about first dates. One of hers involved a funeral. I don't think anything else needs to be said here, while another involved her and a young man sitting as far away as possible from each other and not saying a thing to each other all night. Well, at least no one said anything inappropriate.

My first car date will go down in infamy. The young lady, another couple, and I went to a drive-in. Shortly after arriving, I began to cough and I continued to cough the whole date through. Where this cough came from, I know not, I had not coughed in years prior to that night, but cough I did. The Mistress of the Manor says I was probably nervous. Anyway, I did not ask the girl out again because of my embarrassment, which is okay, because I eventually hooked up with the Mistress of the Manor and have been a blessed man ever since.

Okay, so about this article concerning things a person doesn't say on a first date. I'm writing about dating so as to help anyone out there having trouble making a love connection. Now, this is mainly for older daters, but who knows, maybe the youngsters can also learn a thing or two.

One of the four things you never discuss on a date is your romantic past. Why? Well, if you trash your former girlfriend, it sounds like your aren't over her. If you praise her, it sounds like you aren't over her. If you mention you still talk to her, it sounds like you aren't over her. So keep her out of it. Also, a man should never say something like, "I've slept with 47 women, how many men have you slept with?" If you're a woman, don't say "I've been engaged three times, how about you?" Those are not icebreakers; they're icebergs.

Another thing you don't talk about is kids. Now, it doesn't mean you can't say, "I have a son who's 12 and a daughter who's

10." It means you don't say things like "I have two children I know of," or "I want to have five more kids." Those kinds of comments scare the bejesus out of women. On the other hand, women shouldn't reveal on her first date that Little Elmo has already been arrested more times than he is years old.

When a couple has been together for a while, they may start referring to each other by pet names. For example, I have had numerous pet names for the Mistress of the Manor over the years. Some have been of the normal variety — Honey, Honey Bun, Sweetheart — while others have been, shall we say, more creative — Hotpocket, Puddin' and, the one currently in vogue, Spanky. The Mistress of the Manor, her formal title, by the way, has had some names for me too. We'll just leave it at that. So, unless your date's given name is Sungglebumps, don't call her that on a first date.

The final thing not to talk about on a first date is pets, unless, of course, you two met at a dog show or the pound. No man wants to hear all the cute things Mr. Fluffy Wuffy does, or that Mr. Fluffy Wuffy is his date's barometer for the measure of a man. "I just couldn't be serious about anyone that Mr. Fluffy Wuffy doesn't like" is the kind of thing that will make your date think you are certifiably crazy. Likewise, men, women don't want to hear Sir Barksalot's amazing ability to shred a chair in a matter of minutes, or how many cats he chewed up. One of them might have been her cat.

So, on that first date, keep to the basics. What's your job? What do you like to do for fun — those sorts of things? Never utter a sentence on a first date that includes these words: felony, banned, rape, restraining order, psychiatric hospital, or kill. Sentences to avoid include: "I'm only looking for someone who can financially support me;" "People say I'm conceited, but I just love myself;" "My former boyfriends say that I was too high-maintenance, but I think it's just that they didn't love me enough;" "I'm really into Hitler;" or "I'll be right back. I have to take the biggest dump." Oh, yeah, and always keep a pack of throat lozenges to ward off a surprise coughing attack.

Pageants need a boost

The Mistress of the Manor and I watched the Miss USA Pageant for a little while Sunday night before opting for reading a book and internet Scrabble. Yes, really. Now, I will admit that the part of the pageant we did watch, I probably watched a little bit closer than my beloved of over 40 years so it didn't take me long to tab the deserved winner, but even I grew tired of the silliness of it all.

Let's be honest, once the swimsuit competition is over, the pageant pretty much loses all its pizzazz, at least from the male perspective. I think women like the evening gown competition because of the beautiful dresses. Then there's the intellect section where each young lovely is asked a profound question, such as "Do you prefer your boyfriend to wear boxers or briefs?" If the question is tougher than that, most of the contestants get glassy-eyed, twitch, struggle to answer coherently, and may even drool on themselves.

Who are we kidding here? Does anybody really care what any of the contestants have to say? Well, there might be a few, but, in reality, the question portion of the competition is just a ploy to make viewers believe the pageant is more than a beauty pageant. Yes, a beauty pageant. Of course, the Miss America Pageant is more of the same.

Personally, I think we need to spice up these pageants with some different competitions. One I would suggest, if asked, is called the "Plain Jane" competition. Here, the contestants must appear before the judges and the viewing audience without any makeup or hair styling. That way, we can really see what they're made of. Heck, even with tons of makeup, there are always a couple of girls who beg the question, "Is that the best Nevada can come up with?" There was one contestant Sunday night who looked like Marsha Brady after Bobby hit her in the face with a football.

I would still have the intellect competition, but I would alter it somewhat by having the contestants do tequila shots for three solid hours prior to the pageant. Then I would ask them a question like, "Why is Soren Kierkegaard generally considered the first existentialist philosopher, and do you agree with his philosophy, why or why not?" and let the fun ensue.

Since I noticed Sunday night during a dance number that some of the girls were rhythmically challenged, I think we need a coordination competition. It would have two parts, one, the contestants would have to perform a modern dance, a pole is optional, and, two, they would have to walk the length of the stage in four-inch heels while carrying a tray full of drinks. However, to make this more interesting, once again I would have them do shots three solid hours prior to the show.

I would also have a car parking competition — you can take that however you want — a do-I-pay-the-light-bill-or-buy-the-most-darling-shoes competition, and a how-best-to-get-out-of-a-traffic-ticket competition. These are all important things to know.

I think these changes would not only make the Miss USA and Miss America pageants more interesting, but also give us all a better idea of the contestant's abilities. I mean we don't want just any girl representing this great country; we need to have someone who can handle herself in all situations, sober or drunk.

Driving in the danger zone

I don't know about you, but I love lists. I don't care if it's the best music, the best hotdogs, the best places to visit, the best weasel products (garden weasel, nose weasel, feminine hygiene weasel). I love to read them whether I agree or disagree. After perusing such a list, I may say, "Well done, old chap," or "My good sir, you are dumber than a bag of hammers." Okay, I don't really talk like that. I'm usually more demonstrative, sometimes coarse, vulgar and profane, which draws disapproving looks from the Mistress of the Manor.

Anyway, back to the lists. The first one that caught my eye as I scourged the internet (and we all know how painful that can be) was list of the "Most Dangerous States to Drive In". Now, I try to be a courteous driver, really I do (the Mistress of the Manor is smirking), but I must admit that my anger at drivers who I feel would be better off behind the reins of a hay wagon sometimes gets the best of me.

I worked in North Carolina for 23 years, covering a lot of terrain during that time, so I know the caliber of the motorists there, and felt sure our neighbors to the south would at least make the top 10. The most annoying, and frightening, tactic employed by Tar Heel drivers is the "No, I'm not going, yes I am, but at the last second." Drivers will sit at a stop sign and watch as you approach from a mile away. Only when you get a couple of feet from them will they decide to ease out into traffic, creating fear, anxiety, heart attacks and the occasional wet seat. But did North Carolina make the list? No, siree, that means the 10 that made the list are really a treat.

Six of the top 10 states are southern states, begging the question "What in the name of Henry Ford" is wrong with us. I mean I've been driving 46 years, and have accumulated 10 or so speeding tickets, but never, I repeat never, caused an accident, at least while the car was moving. While I'm amazed and very chagrined to find out my southern brethren apparently have the driving skills of half-blind Pandas, I was even more surprised by two other entries — No.2 Montana and No. 4 Wyoming.

Since those are two of our largest states size-wise, and have a combined population of somewhere around 136 people (I'm pretty sure that's accurate), I'm puzzled by the high death toll. I mean, there are more rabid prairie dogs in those states than there are people. While Mississippi averages 26.7 auto fatalities per 1,000 people to earn the top spot on the list, Montana racked up 23.3 and Wyoming 21.7. Apparently, these people have not transitioned well from the horse to the automobile.

The comments accompanying the list said Montana's "problem may be due in part to drunk driving." Duuuh. Possibly, more horse paths are the answer, or maybe just keeping the firewater away from the guys who have been trampled by bulls and horses one too many times. You've got about the same chance of surviving a trip through Montana as Gen. George Armstrong Custer and his men had surviving the Sioux. While Montana is a puzzler, Wyoming is a Rubic's Cube of wonder. It is huge and has the smallest population of any state in our great country; yet, drivers there manage to kill off themselves and unsuspecting visitors at an alarming rate. What gives? Well, I'll tell you. The fact that Yellowstone National Park is a giant, inactive volcano that could erupt any time and bury half the U.S.A. in volcanic ash has led the state's drivers to adopt a cavalier attitude towards road safety. The state's motto is "Forever West." What state authorities don't tell outsiders is that the forever part might mean death at the hands of a liquored-up wrangler.

And let's not forget Oklahoma, which comes in at the No. 9 spot. In 1974, I had the pleasure — wait, that's not the word — the seemingly unending torment — yea, that's it — to drive the width of the Sooner state. I didn't have to turn the wheel once. It's a straight shot. You could strap a comatose aardvark to the wheel, put a brick on the gas pedal, and that armored maniac would make it to Arkansas (No.5 on the hit list) before crashing into a nursing home.

The other three southern states noted for their ability to produce traffic deaths are third-ranked Alabama, No. 6 South Carolina and No. 10 Kentucky. None of the three require booster seats for children under eight, and South Carolina and Kentucky have no motorcycle helmet laws. So, we have kids and guys undergoing a mid-life crisis bouncing down the pavement, while moonshiners take pot shots at them — fun for the whole family.

The remaining non-south or crazy cowboy state on the list is West Virginia. Need I say anything here? No, not really, but I'm going to. It's hard to drive when you have just one large eye, three ears, and a prehensile tail. Now that I've endeared myself to the people of West Virginia and probably set myself up for a Hatfield/McCoy-type shooting, I'll move on.

I offer this list as a public safety message for all those of you who are planning to travel this summer. If you want to vacation in the Northeast, you're good to go. If the Midwest, West, Southwest, or even the waterlogged Northwest (rethink that one) is your destination, pack up and leave. However, if you have the intention of visiting Georgia or Florida, and the trip doesn't include a boat ride, well then, you're on your own, because you can't get there from here without risking life and limb by traveling through the above mentioned death states. As for the Mistress of the Manor and me, we've already decided not to venture any farther than the "Little Rivera" at Jot'em Down.

Kill them all and let God sort it out

There seems to be a controversy concerning deer stands in Minnesota. Apparently, hunters have taken common deer stands, as we know them, and turned them into mansions of slaughter. While, that is fine with me, county officials seem to be offended by hunters fixing up a little.

Among the items you might find in one of these "mansions" are stairs, decks, shingled roofs, commercial windows, insulation, propane heaters, carpeting, lounge chairs, tables and even generators. All that's missing is a DVD player, and a pole dancer. In addition, some hunters have cut down nearby trees in order to provide better sight lines and planted crops near their stands in order to lure Bambi to his death; which, again, is fine with me.

There was a time when I would be revolted by this, but not anymore. I once thought the bouncing bundles of schizophrenia were cute and a joy to gaze upon. That was before they began their vendetta designed to damage every vehicle the Mistress of the Manor and I have ever owned.

You see, four times deer have leaped into one of our vehicles. Now, you could say I hit the deer, since each time the damage has always been to the front of the vehicle, but, as we all know, deer always instigate the accident. Those tick-infested, energetic bags of vehicular suicide are drawn to a moving vehicle like Charlie Sheen is to hookers.

Our first collision did over $2,000 of damage to our car. I spotted the deer about 100 yards away on top of a steep bank. I said to the Mistress of the Manor, "Look, sweet thang, there's a deer." The next second, we smash into the moldy mound of disease. The second incident with a deer resulted in a totaled vehicle thanks to a slick road, and the deer's fiendish plan to force us into some trees.

The last two incidents have really galled me. The first of the two happened in Cana when a deer collision resulted in damage to a Jeep I had only purchased three months prior. The last incident was the most frustrating since the deer ran out in front of me less than 30 feet from my driveway, damaging the Mistress of the Manor's Cadillac. If she could have caught that deer, she would have ripped out its heart and ate it. Okay, that may be a little dramatic, but she would have broken its legs and left it to be eaten alive by whatever vermin stumbled upon it.

As you might expect, we have become very wary of the four-footed furry devils, but it is hard for us to avoid them. Although we live in the town limits, our area is heavily wooded, and deer often graze in our yard, especially when the acorns are falling. They walk by our front porch while we're sitting there. They listen to the Mistress of the Manor scold them about eating her flowers. They just stare at us, like we're the intruders. If they had fingers, I'm sure they would give us one.

To be honest, I am ready to gun down ever white-tailed, big-eyed bundle of destruction I see. I hate deer with a passion, so I have no problem with hunters being comfortable while preparing for the kill. However, a kill shot seems much too good for the quick-footed, dull-witted maniacs of mayhem. I think torture is in order; maybe dragging them to the highway and slowly running over their legs with an automobile, or maybe slowly driving a screwdriver into their ear with a hammer, or maybe taking a blowtorch to — okay, I'm getting carried away.

Although deer are my main bane of animal torment, recently another feral creature has drawn my distain — the opossum. Yeah, that's right, that diseased critter of ugliness. Coming back from Martinsville one night, an opossum scurried into our path. Now, I've run over an opossum before without any problem. However, this wasn't just any ordinary opossum. That rascal somehow managed to rip a loose a large, hard rubber something-or-other that protects the underside of the engine from road debris. I finally found a place with some outside lights so I could pull over and fix the damage. Luckily, I had some rope in the trunk and was able to tie one end of the rope to the something-or-other while holding the other end of the rope in my left hand. When I reported this strange occurrence to my insurance agent, she said I wasn't her first customer to suffer opossum damage. She added that she had even had a claim on damage caused by a rabbit, which, after being struck, had flown up and busted out a headlight.

It used to be, you only had to worry about deer. Now, we know opossums and rabbits are threatening our driving safety. What next? Will the raccoons get into the act? Will groundhogs take up kamikaze missions? Will the weasels join the fray? I hope not, those weasels can be treacherous creatures. It's got to the point that I get on edge any time I see a woodland creature near one of our vehicles. The other day, I saw two chipmunks crouched next to my Jeep; and let me tell you, they were up to no good. Chip and Dale, they were not.

Remembering Halloween

Well, tonight's the big night. Yea, all the ghoulies, beasties and things that go bump in the night will be roaming the streets of Hillsville. Treats will be plentiful, and young and old monsters alike will have a happy, and most importantly safe, Halloween. But, there's always a *but*. Safe is good, but I can't help feel that today's zombies are missing out on the fun we had as kids roaming these very same streets.

Back in the long-long-ago-before-time of my youth, kids could traverse the streets of this small burg without any real danger. Sure, you might get your candy stolen, or hit with an egg or water balloon, but that was part of the excitement, raking in the loot while avoiding the danger posed by the older kids. The good thing was that you would eventually become an older kid who posed the threat, not only to younger kids, but also to adults. Before leaving for a night of frivolity, you would make sure you had all the prerequisites — the aforementioned eggs and water balloons, as well as toilet paper and several small bags of manure. Now, most people usually went with manure of cow, since that was the most common in these parts. Others used dog manure or horse manure. I, personally, favored pig manure. I always felt it had the right mixture of stickiness, odor and color for the perfect Halloween surprise.

Anyway, we would sit the bag of manure in front of someone's door, light it on fire, knock on the door or ring the doorbell, then hightail it out of there. When they opened the door and saw a flaming bag, they would naturally begin to stomp on it, which resulted in a very messy shoe; and, in some cases, singed clothing and leg hair. The water balloons were primarily for other creatures of the night, and eggs were good for a variety of targets – kids, houses, cars, and pets. The toilet paper, of course, was useful in adding that distinct decorating touch to the landscaping of a home.

In fact, it was while a group of us were involved in said landscaping that we got more trick than we had bargained for. We were quiet, or so we thought, TP-ing the yard of our favorite coach. You only TP the ones you love. There were no lights on in the house, so we thought we were good to go. We had just begun to decorate when a shotgun blast went off right behind us. Needless to say, we had plenty of manure at that point. Coach had a good laugh about that one, but youth has its advantages, so as soon as he tired and went to bed, we did possibly the best job of TP landscaping in the history of Halloween. The mischief lasted until late in the night, or rather, the early morning hours and sometimes not until our town police officer said enough was enough.

Eventually, everybody outgrows the trick phase of Halloween — okay, everybody except for Rooster Edwards — and you become an adult, or you at least attempt to act like an adult, although that can be hard to do at Halloween. Then all those years of tormenting others comes back to haunt you. Now, I've never stomped on a bag of burning manure, but our vehicles have been egged and our yard has been landscaped with toilet paper, especially when the Mistress of the Manor was teaching. Students TP-ing teachers' yards, is just as natural as Mitt Romney outsourcing jobs.

However, there is something very interesting about adults when it comes to Halloween, and it involves the infamous costume parties. One thing I, along with most men, find very interesting about Halloween is women will wear outfits to Halloween parties that they normally wouldn't wear in their own bedroom. Another thing is men will wear outfits at Halloween that would normally get them drummed out of the Jaycees. Once when I was a young lad, my uncle, all 230 pounds of him, showed up at our house wearing just a sheet tied in the fashion of a diaper. Did he just show up dressed that way for our amusement? No, he was headed to a Halloween Dance at the VFW. A friend of the Mistress of the Manor once showed up at school, which was having costume day, wearing a nurse's outfit with stains on the knees of her white stockings. Was she just a nurse with dirty stockings? No, she was a head nurse. It seems her costume was inspired by her doctor husband's decision to leave her for one of his nurses.

Although the Mistress of the Manor and I have donned costumes at times, we usually don't dress up at Halloween, mainly because she says I provide enough strangeness on a day-to-day basis. Instead, we watch our beloved "Rocky Horror Picture Show," along with some real horror movies, play scrabble and eat popcorn. Yes, I know, that does sound exciting.

Now, you may ask why I waited to write about Halloween so late. It is, after all, tonight. Well, I did so out of a civic responsibility. If I had written this a week earlier, there would have been time for some young person to peruse it and get some ideas. I hear TP landscaping is still in vogue, but for the life of me I can't remember when I last heard about someone finding a flaming bag of manure (other than Rush Limbaugh) on their doorstep. And I think we need to keep it that way.

If you're looking for a job, try one of these

A lot of people are struggling in today's economy, so in an effort to help my fellow citizens, I've been doing some research into the job market. Although the market has improved since the crash of September, 2008, good jobs are still not overly abundant. Now, this advice will be more valuable to young people than to old spits like me, but after all, they are our future; at least until December 21 when most of us become post-apocalyptic zombies.

However, there is still a chance that the Mayans were either playing a cruel joke on future inhabitants, or the guy — I think his name was Fuyu — decided to take an extended banana break with his sweetie pie, Fume, and forgot to finish the calendar. With that in mind, I hope this mortal coil will still be turning on Dec. 22. Still, there may be zombies.

So if we do not have a zombie apocalypse, these are some good-paying jobs young non-zombies should look into. Before I go any further, it's not that I'm prejudiced against zombies, it's just that their smell and the limbs-falling-off thing gets on co-workers' nerves. And, of course, the highest-paying jobs can only be had by people with the first name of Lawrence, Freeman, Halston or Punjab.

One of the best good-paying jobs available, according to some fly-by-night career advice website I stumbled on, is that of being a registered nurse. Now, this job pays around $61,000 a year, but there is a downside. You have to deal with sick people, who can be pretty annoying with all their moaning, crying and habit of excreting bodily fluids at inappropriate times. And sometimes, they're much like zombies, in that things fall off.

Number two on the list is certified public accountant. This job also pays around $61,000 a year, but it also has a drawback – numbers. You have to be very good with numbers to be an accountant, and very creative with numbers if you're working for an insurance company, which is much like a mob family in that accountants who can't maneuver numbers to fit their bosses' needs, are dealt with severely.

Auditor comes in at number three on the list, and what do auditors do? Well, they evaluate a company's finances and check for fraud. If you want to be successful at this job, the trick here is to find any fraud committed by employees, but ignore the fraud committed by the CEO.

Next up on the list is facilities director, which has a nice sound to it. Your friend asks, "What do you do for a living?" "Oh, I'm the facilities director at Armbrister Enterprises," you reply. Your friend is impressed until he finds out that Armbrister makes inflatable sheep for discriminating adults. A drawback to the job is you have to keep an eye on virtually every aspect of the business. So, if a water line bursts or the plant loses power during third shift, you have to be there to deal with the crisis.

Operations manager is next on the list, and is much like the facilities director, except you must also deal with the public in the area of sales and customer service. If one of those pesky customers gets upset because the inflatable sheep he purchased did not make it through one petting session, you have to find out why, calm the customer's anger and find out why your company is making subpar inflatable sheep.

The job of payroll manager deals with paying employees, reporting taxes, and things like that. One of those things like that is sometimes called "skimming." Now, skimming can prove be to very lucrative if you're good at it, and make it to the Cayman Islands before the boss finds out about it. However, you can also end up in prison sharing a cell with a monster of a man named Belch, who refers to you as Nancy.

The list is rounded off with automobile salesman. Now, I know this job lends itself to many jokes, but these guys have to work hard for their money, much like another profession. I mean, it's not easy to convince someone why the 2001 Focus you're pushing costs more than the new Cadillac at the rival dealer across the street, or why that grinding sound they hear when pressing on the brakes is really of no concern. The job takes creativity, persistence and determination. I, however, couldn't do this job; not because of the aforementioned required attributes, but because I hate white loafers.

As for these jobs, I admit I could do none of those with enthusiasm or competency. I'm not meant to take care of sick people, analyze numbers or fix things (just ask the Mistress of the Manor about that one). No, I'm meant to do what I do – expose the public to all the real and made-up information I can cram into this 20 or so inches of copy. That is my calling in life; to inform and to misinform, to entertain and to annoy. However, if any zombie killing jobs open up, I'm all in.

We don't need no stinkin' Texas

I guess, by now, most of you know a much of bozos in Texas want to secede from the union. Yes, they want to take their cows, oil and death penalty, and become a country of their own. Can Texas really do that you may ask? Well, according to numerous authorities, it can't. But legalities aren't something that Texans are all that concerned about.

Although Texas has made the most news about seceding, there have been many prior failed attempts in the recent past. There have been at least eight since 1998, when some yahoo in Maryland decided that the eastern shore of that state, as well as parts of Delaware and Virginia, should secede to form the great state of — get ready for it — Delmarva. This idea was hatched by State Senator Richard Colburn, who proposed that the mushroom to be the state flower, the state fungi and the state bird. It seems to me that someone likes mushrooms a little too much.

Pima County in Arizona thought it would be better off on its own in 2011, but came up short in trying to establish Baja Arizona, while some maple syrup guzzlers in the southern part of Maine wanted to form their own state of Northern Massachusetts. Just last year, one legislator in West Virginia wanted to allow the panhandle counties of the state to secede and rejoin Virginia, which promptly began building an electrified fence along its border.

Secession attempts have surfaced in Utah, Tennessee, Rhode Island and New York. In fact, New York may own the record. One attempt would have made the state of New York a country, another would have done so for New York City, and still another would have created the state of Long Island. It was rumored that if Long Island succeeded, Billy Joel would have almost assuredly been named king.

Okay, now let's get back to Texas, which has received the signatures of over 100,000 people on an online petition. Although most of the names are thought to be those of Texas residents, there is a chance that more than a few belong to residents of Oklahoma, which would love to see Texas out of the picture. Now, one reason, according to leader of the secession movement, why Texas needs to secede from the U.S. is our country's huge deficit. Strangely, enough when President George W. Bush, the former Texas governor, was turning a surplus into a huge deficit, there was no talk of secession. Methinks there are other reasons behind the movement, and they ain't pretty.

If Texas, which was a republic for a decade before joining the United States, did secede, it could then split into five states of its own. How in the name of Sam Houston could this happen? Well, in the legislation that added Texas to the union in 1845, it gave Texas the right to do so. I mean, we could have North Texas, West Texas, East Texas, South Texas, and, of course, Austin Texas, where Texas now hides all its liberals.

Historians, such as retired professor Herb Arbuckle, say Texas can't legally secede. Sean P. Cunningham, a professor at Texas Tech University, agrees. In fact, no one is taking this talk seriously except those yahoos in Texas.

After giving it some serious thought, I've come to the conclusion that maybe we should let Texas secede. Then, we invade Mexico and take it into the union, thereby solving all this fuss about immigration. Now, that we have Texas almost surrounded, we establish a trade embargo and a naval blockade to prevent any goods from going in or coming out of Texas.

Some of you out there probably think this is a little crazy — okay; a lot crazy, but we must keep the union together. "A house divided will not stand," said President Abraham Lincoln. So if some of you other states get a little jumpy, you had better think twice. There's ways of dealing with turncoats. I've always thought that Utah would make a nice penal colony.

Danger science

If you're like me, when you think of scientists, you think white coats, broken glasses and mouse molesting. However, after stumbling across an article — don't worry, I wasn't hurt — about danger scientists, I have a new respect for the bundles of inquisitiveness. Yes, as it turns out, some of these guys and gals live on the wild side and flirt with danger, although seldom with the opposite sex.

The article I read listed seven danger scientists, but I'm just going to deal with a few of this strange breed, beginning with venom- milkers. Yes, that's right venom-milkers. Now, I don't find these guys as strange as some others, because I've liked to catch snakes since I was a young lad. I'll be honest with you, though, I've never caught a poisonous snake in the wild, although I've tried.

One time a relative from West Virginia — please don't spread it around that I have relatives in the toothless state — came to visit and with him was a rattlesnake he had captured on the Blue Ridge Parkway. Since he hadn't anticipated the availability of a snake, he put it in the only container he had, an empty gas can. By the time my relative — make that unknown stranger — transferred the snake to a crate, it was very drunk on gas fumes. Every time it tried to coil up into striking position, it would fall over. I felt this was the perfect opportunity to handle a rattlesnake, but my parents nixed that idea, saying something like, "Who you think you are, a scientist?

Years later, helping put up hay on my grandfather's farm gave me plenty of opportunities to handle copperheads. The first time I took time off from work to catch one of the buggers, my grandfather told me we were in the business of putting up hay, not catching snakes, then promptly killed it. We would kill at least one copperhead a day and sometimes two during those all so much fun days putting up hay.

Some 30 years ago, the Mistress of the Manor and I were headed to Fox Hunter's Paradise for a company outing. As we neared our destination, we saw a snake crossing the road, and to my excitement, it was a rattlesnake. I pleaded for her to pull the car over and she eventually did. I found I could get within about two feet of the snake before it would begin to coil. I would take a step back and the snake would attempt to make his escape; a step forward and the snake would begin to coil. I yelled to the Mistress of the Manor to find me a stick so I could pin its head down and grab it. She refused; she can be like that sometimes. Anyways, I eventually had to let the snake crawl off into the grass to eat a mouse or bite somebody.

Another danger scientist is the cave diver, who I think are really crazy. I'd much rather attempt to catch a rattlesnake than to go cave diving. Quite honestly, I'm not big on dry caves. I think they're beautiful and amazing, but the whole time I'm in one, I expecting to be crushed or trapped by a cave-in, or, quite possibly, attacked by Sleestaks. Add water to a cave situation and you've got even bigger trouble. If you think I am being unnecessarily timid, think about this, from 1969 through 2007, 368 Americans died while cave diving. Some of them, I think, were eaten by a Megaladon.

Then we have the crocodile physiologist, who stands to get eaten by one of those giant creatures so popular on the SyFy Channel. Physiologists study function in living systems. I'm not even a physiologist and I can tell you what the function of a crocodile is — to eat you! This one group of psychos, I mean physiologists, would jump into crocodile-infested water at night to study these magnificent creatures. Something about that seems like a bad idea.

I saved the most dangerous danger scientist for last — the lab technician. Now, you may ask, "What in the name of Marie Currie is he talking about?" Working in a lab may not seem dangerous, but all kinds of awful things can happen. When experiments go wrong, there are often horrible results. You can get burnt or shocked; you can end up with a prehensile tail or an extra butt crack, or even turn into a ghastly creature like Zombie Joe or Rush Limbaugh.

Now, I know firsthand about the dangers involved. I experienced some rather strange happenings during one of my stints as an amateur lab technician during my college years. One time, after a particularly intriguing experiment, I thought me, Salvador Dali and Bob Dylan were riding a winged chipmunk through a forest of giant Petunias. I think we were headed to Middle Earth or, possibly, Funky Town, I'm not sure. Anyway, a few hours later I realized that was just a side effect of my lab work. However, I still have a prehensile tail.

Supreme Court may look at boobies

The U.S. Supreme Court, which has ruled on such important issues as race and gender discrimination, abortion, and gay marriage, may soon be taking on the subject of boobies. Let that sink in. The highest court in the land may soon be discussing boobies.

I hope they rule in favor of boobies, but with this Supreme Court, there's no telling what decision it will render. After all, this court has struck down a series of campaign finance restrictions, which have drowned out the voice of the common man in favor of the wealthy. So, what they may do if boobies show up on the court docket is uncertain.

Now, to be honest, the court won't be discussing boobies per se; however, they will be discussing what role boobies have in high school. Okay, that's not exactly right, heck, we all know what role boobies have in high school. No, they will be discussing if it's okay for boobies to be used to promote breast cancer awareness.

A couple of years ago two girls in Pennsylvania decided to challenge their school district's ban on bracelets which read "I (heart) boobies," by wearing them to school. The bracelets are designed to promote breast cancer awareness among young people. The bracelets, you see, work especially well with young people since girls want boobies and boys like to look at boobies. It's a win-win.

Well, the school board forbid the girls from wearing the bracelets, saying the bracelets were lewd, so the girls sued with help from an attorney from the American Civil Liberties Union, which can always be counted on to defend boobies. Much to the school board's chagrin, the girls won. The school board appealed the decision, but once again was shot down; this time in federal court, which upheld the lower court decision.

So now, the school board is thinking it might just have to take the case to the highest court in the land to prevent these two little perverts from spreading their filth. Superintendent John Reinhardt told the media the bracelets were "cause-based marketing energized by sexual double-entendres." Well, look at the brain on John Reinhardt.

School district solicitor John Freund said the National School Boards Association and others are "concerned about the implications of a hyper-sexualized environment." I need to address two things here. One, what the hell is a school district solicitor? That sounds pretty darn suspicious to me.

Secondly, it's high school; of course, there's a hyper-sexualized environment, although it wasn't always that way. Prior to 60s when sex was discovered, boys and girls went on their merry way, sipping sodas at the malt shop and talking about the big game. No one talked about boobies.

However, along came the turbulent 60s and talk turned to boobies and all kinds of things. There were even bra burnings, which I fully supported. Of course, nowadays with all the twerking that's going on, I really don't think bracelets that read "I (heart) boobies" are really going to make the atmosphere any more sexually charged than it already is. If we are to ban something, I think it should be Miley Cyrus.

Just recently a local group trying to raise awareness of breast cancer used the slogan "Howling for Hooters" to publicize its event. Its backup slogan was "Save Second Base." Those seem more sexually charged than "I (heart) boobies" do, which seems rather harmless, sort of like you are talking about puppies.

Besides if the bracelets make just a few young people more aware of the seriousness of breast cancer, makes them realize boobies are more than just objects to be highlighted by laser pointers, the bracelets have done their job. So I say, school board members forget this silly idea of taking this matter to the Supreme Court and learn to love the boobies.

Made in the USA
Middletown, DE
10 January 2015